D1282112

THERE'S MONEY IN PICTURES

BY LEO M. SOLOMON

Chief, Press Photo Unit, Photographic Branch, International Information Program, Department of State; former Editor, Wide World Photos of the New York *Times* and of The Associated Press

There's Money in Pictures

A NEWSWEEK BOOK

PUBLISHED FOR *NEWSWEEK*

NEW YORK : : : *FUNK & WAGNALLS COMPANY*

TO

F. Z. S.

PRINTED IN THE UNITED STATES OF AMERICA
1

Foreword

IF IT WEREN'T FOR THE FACT THAT CUSTOM requires a book to have a foreword, these few paragraphs would not be here. For, in the words of the toastmaster, "the next speaker needs no introduction." Just mention the name of Leo Solomon among any gathering of editors who've had the slightest acquaintance with news pictures, and you'll get a nod of recognition and a smile of approval from all. And may I supplement this by saying that, in my belief, "Solomon" and "pictures" should be listed in the dictionaries as synonyms?

Somewhere on the jacket, undoubtedly, the publisher of this book will have a brief résumé of Mr. Solomon's connections and achievements in the picture world. This, I am confident, will be a modest appraisal. Many of his feats in this none too sane business are stored in the secret treasure house of his mind. Leo Solomon is not given to self-approbation.

It has been said on occasion, and truthfully so, I think, that writers of prefaces sometimes have not read the books for which they have written glowing introductions. Not here. I have scanned every line of this book, not only with pleasure, but also with profit. I was able to pick up buried nuggets, despite my thirty years of daily association with news and feature pictures. That either proves Mr. Solomon knows the business inside out, or else I haven't been very observant during my years of picture handling. Or maybe it's a case of you're never too old to learn.

I was particularly appreciative of Mr. Solomon's words of caution—his deflation of great expectations of fortunes to be made in the sale of pictures. But, in this thoroughly readable and authoritative book, he certainly shows the way to get the most out of your picture product. As a matter of simple economics, the amateur photographer just can't lose on an investment in *There's Money in Pictures.* He'll make up the cost of it in short order, if he has anything worthwhile to sell. And he'll get a further dividend in merely reading the book for pleasure.

William J. White, Jr.
Picture Editor,
The Daily News, New York

By Way of Acknowledgment

THIS IS A VERY PLEASANT PART OF PUTTING A book together: the opportunity to thank publicly those who have helped.

The first thank-you goes to Dorothy Woolf of NEWSWEEK. Her cooperation in editing this volume was invaluable. She read and assayed every word. At least this once, a writer has no complaint against the copy desk. Quite often she found the better word to say what I meant.

All through, from the first outline, the help and suggestions of Tom Malley of NEWSWEEK have kept me on the right path. He was my advocate in working with the publisher as I turned in copy and pictures.

To Tom Maloney of *U. S. Camera* go my thanks for making the original suggestion that I do a book on this subject. Joseph E. Lowes, Jr., who was present on that occasion, is the good godfather who christened this volume.

I take this opportunity, too, for public acknowledgment of help from Victor W. Talley and Emile Barriere of the New York *Times;* William J. White, Jr., Ben Handel, and George Schmidt of the New York *Daily News;* Robert Dorman, Harry Cohen, Harold Blumenfeld, and Eleanor Ohsol of Acme Newspictures; F. A. Resch, Murray Becker, Kenneth Lucas, Carl D. Nesensohn, and Ruby Weil of Associated Press and its affiliate, Wide World Photos; Richard Sarno of Hearst Newspapers, and Sid Mautner of International News Photos; also Dorothy Hoover, Natalie Kosek, Mary Carr, Ruth Lester, and the staff of the Picture Bureau of *Life;* Sam Kaufman of the National Broadcasting Company, Joseph J. Wurzel of *Look*, and James A. Quigney of

Collier's; John J. Winterich, Charles E. Cushing, Frank O. Seed, Con Gebbie, Frances De Marquis, Russ Countryman, Bill Sharpe, Charles and Lucile Herbert, Robin Garland, and Harold Farkas.

I am grateful also to those four pioneers of aerial news photography, Charles McLaughlin, Capt. Robert Smith, Col. Victor Dallin, and Virgil Kauffman.

A great debt is owed to all the editors and photographers who were kind enough to talk to me or write the answers to questions. Without their replies this book would have been a bare skeleton.

The final thank-you goes to all the photographers, professional, free-lance, and amateur, who have taught me what little I know of the photographic trade. To them I say, "Picture editors' reputations are made on your feats and the wonderful photographs you produce." I thank you.

LEO M. SOLOMON

Contents

FOREWORD, v
by William J. White, Jr., of the New York *Daily News*

BY WAY OF ACKNOWLEDGMENT, vii

INTRODUCTION, 3

CASH IN ON SPOT NEWS, 10

FUN AND PROFIT IN FEATURES, 20

GOING UP IN THE AIR FOR PICTURES, 39

CAPTIONS SELL PICTURES, 65

SELLING TO THE PICTURE SERVICES, 75

WHAT THE NEWSPAPERS WANT, 97

THE MARKET IN THE MAGAZINES, 128

THE "LITTLE" MARKETS, 150

TIPS FROM THE PROFESSIONALS, 168

THEY WERE THERE WHEN NEWS WAS BREAKING, 183

INDEX, 197

Pictures

At page 182

The Winecoff Hotel fire – Pulitzer Prize picture
The *Vestris* disaster – opportunity in tragedy
The Esposito (mad dog) killings – cameraman's luck
Seconds from eternity – captured time
The Staten Island Ferry Terminal fire – vacationer's jackpot
Helicopter rescue at Niagara Falls – special-market picture
Another Empire State Building suicide – photography student's chance
Eclipse of the moon – planned success
Seeding the desert from the air – quiet drama
A ship in every slip – a steady seller
The church by the roadside – a study in composition
Picturing sleep in an airplane – lighting: right and wrong
A bull elephant ready to charge – split-second timing
The Associated Press Wirephoto Network
Acme Telephoto Network
INP Sound Photo System

THERE'S MONEY IN PICTURES

Introduction

ANYONE WHO OWNS A CAMERA has an excellent chance to make money by turning opportunities for news pictures into cash. There is only one catch to getting salable news photographs; the cameraman must be on the spot when and where news is breaking.

There is no question that the staff photographers of newspapers, press associations, and magazines have the advantage when it comes to prearranged events. They have the right of way at public functions, sporting events, and the thousand and one routine happenings that are pictured in the press. But they have no advantage of advance information over the veriest tyro when it comes to events of unexpected occurrence. And in the field of news feature photography their advantage of experience is often overbalanced by the fresh approach of the non-professional photographer.

Your chance of being on the spot when automobiles collide, trains run off the track, a building catches fire or topples over, and the like, are at least as good as the pro's. It may even be better, because between jobs, professional news photographers are normally in their offices awaiting assignments while you are outdoors going about your business. In my days on picture desks a crystal ball that could have told us where to send photographers to wait for news to break would have been most welcome. Fortunately for every free-lance with a camera workable and efficient, such crystal balls haven't been invented.

The main requirement for making your camera produce a cash return is to be where the news is. Metropolitan newspapers, especially picture tabloids like the *Daily News* and *Mirror* in New York and the Los Angeles *Mirror*, pay well for on-the-spot pictures. Keep in mind that the news itself need not be always of major importance. A striking photograph of a minor hold-up just around the corner from you, if made at the crux of action, should have more dramatic value and may get wider use than an after-the-fact picture of the scene of a major robbery. Newspapers are not the only market for spot-news pictures; the leading press associations are constantly seeking good photographs of spot-news happenings.

Mind you, I would not recommend that anyone chuck his or her job to try for a living as a free-lance photographer. There are very few who earn their keep at that precarious calling. Most of the free-lances depend for their livelihood upon assignments from periodicals and advertising agencies. In fact most of the so-called top-flight free-lance cameramen are really devoting full time to one of the divisions of commercial photography, whether or not they work alone or maintain well-rounded organizations. In more than thirty years in various selling and editorial phases of news photography, I have met very few who made a consistent living by free-lancing for newspapers and press associations.

The tips in this book on how to make photography pay cash dividends are intended for two large and growing classes of cameramen. The first group comprises all you enthusiasts who make pictures for the fun of it. Every amateur knows he makes some photos worthy of publication and would like to see them printed. Getting paid for his pictures, as well as seeing them widely used, should add an extra thrill.

The other group includes all the professional cameramen who have by-passed news photography as a losing proposition. If they are thinking of it as a full-time occupation, we agree with their conclusion. But if a little consideration in the right direction is applied to the problem, selling photographs to newspapers, press associations, magazines, house organs, etcetera, can be developed into a very profitable sideline. A knowledge of publication needs and how best to present your pictures for each market can turn spare photographs from routine studio or commercial jobs into welcome extra cash.

We can't tell you how to find out in advance when your local bank will be held up. But we can tell you how to proceed if you and your camera should happen to be around when the hold-up occurs. For hobbyists and professionals alike, we can offer some guidance on caption writing, on making feature pictures, and on how to submit photographs for publication, outlining also some of the differences in procedure required in dealing with the various types of publications. There is a vast difference, too, between the urgency required in speeding pictures of spot-news events to the likeliest buyer and the leisurely, but not too leisurely, painstaking approach that brings greatest return for feature offerings.

Since our theme is marketing, not producing, photographs, we are deliberately keeping away from the technicalities of photography. We assume that you have a camera and are reasonably expert in its manipulation. If you aren't, we suggest that you study and practice until you are fairly adept before you seek a market for your pictures.

The only pointers on cameras we will offer are newspaper and press-association preferences on size. These are not absolute standards. They are simply the sizes which in most darkrooms can be handled most efficiently and speedily. In negatives the preferred size range is from 4 by 5 inches down to 2¼ by 2¼. If the pictures are clear and sharp, most purchasers are not much concerned with the equipment that produced it. The pay-off is for results, whether you are using an old box camera with a single segment lens or the latest model press camera complete with all attachments. And if the news is hot enough, any negative size from a single movie frame up will find acceptance. To a lesser degree, variation in print size is allowable. Glossies on 7 by 9 and on 8 by 10 inch paper are standard, but there is no bar to larger or smaller sizes. Often, subject and shipping conditions govern print size.

To be ready for spot-news breaks, be sure that your camera is always loaded with film. And keep it close by you all the time. If you get around by automobile, you will not be as limited on the size of equipment as the person moving about afoot. In any event it pays to have the best outfit you can afford, both in price and the amount of bulk you can tote. A good speed flash attachment is practically standard nowadays, and you will need it if you seek news shots. The exact type of outfit you buy should be decided on the basis of your ability to use its potentialities, the results you are seeking, the weight of both camera and attachments that is comfortable, and the price you can afford to pay.

Maybe you are not as concerned with the financial returns as with getting your picture published. That's all right too. Photographs are made to be shown. Publication increases the number of persons who will see your work. Whatever your ultimate aim, the procedure toward publication is basically the same.

All photographers feel that their favorite pictures should be published. They are very unselfish in thinking that a wider audience than friends and relatives should enjoy the beauty they catch with the camera. Sometimes the cameraman is right, but more often he is wrong. It takes more than sharp focus, proper exposure, and fair composition to produce a news photograph worthy of publication.

Looking back over the years, we rather sadly recall that most of the unsolicited photographs that came across our desk should never have been submitted. The photographer not only wasted his own time and money, but ours too. If we can help you decide what to submit and what to discard, this volume will achieve a good deal of its purpose. You should have some definite news standards besides your own pride of creation and the advice of well-meaning friends who are prone to say: "That's much better than the picture — printed last week. Why don't you send your photo to them?"

We shall try, for your sake, and for the sake of the editors on the receiving end, to set up some guideposts. Don't be discouraged if some of them read Stop. Too many Go signs might tempt you to waste too much time and money. Submitting pictures without careful and discriminating appraisal is bad business. Editors are anxious to see fresh contributions, but they soon tire of examining pictures from people who show they don't know what the publication wants. To make certain that editors don't tag you as a careless contributor whose material isn't worth inspecting, feel your way carefully. Don't be disappointed by rejections. That's part of the game. Studying rejections should help you find out what a publication is interested in. And often material rejected by one editor will find ready acceptance from another. There is wide variation among publication requirements. Just as you allowed for trial and error when you began to take pictures, be equally as patient while you learn to sell them.

The market for news photographs is broad. There has been some shrinkage in certain directions, but on the whole it is expanding. There may be fewer newspapers now than formerly, but those that are left use more pictures. And the number of periodicals using photographs is growing constantly. We cannot mention all picture markets within the confines of this book. Some are so specialized that only a very few would be interested in aiming at such narrow fields. Others require full-time concentration to meet their demands, and we are limiting discussion to opportunities for cashing in on sideline efforts. Others offer too little in cash or other reward in return for the effort required to cultivate them. We shall instead try to cover the wide market that exists among newspapers, press associations, periodicals, house organs, and the like. They offer the best chance of profiting from extra-curricular photographic activity.

For the purposes of this book, then, we are assuming that every reader knows his camera, that he is reasonably expert in handling it, and that he can turn out a good negative when he runs into a newsworthy subject. We are assuming, too, that his knowledge of news is not that of the professional but is that of the average newspaper reader. And we assume that he lacks the experience in selling news photographs that would tell him where he can get the most acceptances and highest prices. Hence we shall canvass the picture market, outlining its varied requirements, and explaining how best to fulfil them.

Perhaps before we go farther we should define what we mean by news pictures as opposed to news feature pictures. Though there may be some slight overlapping of fields, we shall understand each other if we define as "spot news" almost all pictures of an actual news event. That would cover pictures made of disasters, earthquakes, fires, murders, battlefields, sports events, governmental doings, war preparation, speeches, political and other conventions, ship and plane departures, Congressional hearings, and the rest of the everyday grist of normal and abnormal living.

We will consider as features those photographs in which the telling of a story is the principal purpose and result, and for which neither timeliness nor the event itself is of paramount importance. Obviously the cameraman's approach to and treatment of the subject are the principal ingredients in producing usable feature pictures. The element of luck has only minor effect. For the most part, the best feature photographers create their own opportunities. Often a resourceful and imaginative cameraman will produce an outstanding feature picture or a whole series from a fresh approach to some routine news event. More often features will be created from happenings that originally lacked all semblance to news.

The primary need of newspapers and press associations is for pictures of actual events made by cameramen who were right there when the events occurred. The papers want such pictures fast. Prices paid will vary upward in direct relation to the importance of the news pictured and the speed with which the cameraman delivers his photographs. Many magazines want news photographs also, but, unless the publications are right up to deadlines, the need for speed is not so great. Newspapers, press associations, and magazines are all interested in the so-called feature news pictures. Usually features require a series of shots, but often a single picture will turn out to be a good feature. In this book there will be entire chapters devoted to spot news and to feature pictures.

As we get into the subject, we will recount some outstanding examples of photographers' cashing in handsomely through luck, backed up by more or less preparation in advance. Readiness is twofold; it consists not only of having a camera you know how to use but also of checking sources in advance to learn where to send your pictures to get the best return.

The only advantage the professionals have over the amateurs is experience, and that isn't much compared with the luck of being at the right place at the right time. Many amateurs have done as well or better. Everyone old enough to have been looking at newspapers in 1928 remembers the famous photographs of the milling passengers on the sloping deck of the sinking *Vestris.* These were made by a steward who had no trouble selling them. All he had to do was to turn his film over to the highest bidder when reporters and cameramen met the survivors in New York Harbor. Camera-conscious sailors aboard one of our naval vessels cashed in handsomely during the war when their ship came into New York after rescuing the crew of the scuttled Nazi steamer *Columbus.* We knew one ship's steward on a passenger liner shuttling back and forth between New York and Bermuda who did so well with his camera that he quit the sea to open a studio on that British island.

You may have luck in making photographs as dramatic as any of these; you may find yourself interested in the creation of features; or you may already have in your files photographs that are salable because they can be used as illustrations. If this book helps you to market such output, it will have achieved its purpose.

Cash in on Spot News

YOU WANT TO SELL PICtures, or you wouldn't be reading this book. As we have pointed out, there is a large element of chance in making money from spot-news photography. But it isn't all chance. You yourself can do a number of things to nudge Lady Luck along.

Primarily you must always be ready to take advantage of the good fortune of being in the right spot when big news is breaking. To be ready, there are only two things you must do—but both are important. Overlooking one or the other may be very costly.

First, never go anywhere without your complete photographic outfit. Second—and do this right now or as soon as you have finished this chapter—canvass your local situation so that when you do make a spot-news picture you will know right away where you can most readily sell it and how best to send it to that market.

This land of ours is too broad for us to draw a plan of action that will be adequate everywhere. Obviously the rules that will govern for photographers in metropolitan centers like New York, Washington, Chicago, San Francisco, Los Angeles, and Denver, to mention a few, might not work well in Sweetwater, Texas, or Staunton, Virginia. In big towns and small there will be variations from town to town.

You can start by learning the names and addresses of the nearest metropolitan newspapers. While you are doing that, also find out the addresses of the nearest bureaus of the three major press associations, each of which has its own news-photo affiliate—the Associated Press, the United Press (Acme), and International News Service (International News Photos). If you can't get the bureau addresses from nearby sources, write to their headquarters. All three are in New York City. Associated Press News Photos Service is at 50 Rockefeller Plaza, New York 20, Acme News Pictures at 461 Eighth Avenue, New York 1, and International News Photos at 225 East 45th Street, New York 17. In each case, address your inquiry to the Editor.

Unless you know someone on the staff, don't make personal calls on the picture editors of press associations or metropolitan newspapers. That applies even if they are in the same town or very close to your city. Editors are much too rushed to welcome interruptions. They would prefer that you write. Usually you will get a prompt reply. If you don't, you will know one place that is not a good market for your spot-news picture offerings.

We suggest that your inquiry be brief and to the point. Here is a draft that you can modify to meet your own needs:

> Dear Mr. ....:
>
> Is the .... in the market for spot-news picture contributions from free-lance photographers? I am an amateur (a professional) photographer living in ....
>
> If you are interested, please tell me the procedure to follow in getting hot news photographs to you. I am enclosing a few prints (negatives) so you may judge technical proficiency.
>
> My home address is .... The business address is ...., and the telephone number is ....
>
> Sincerely yours,

Change the wording to suit yourself but don't make the letter any longer. You can use the same basic form in writing both to the press associations and the newspapers you may want to contact. Before you write, try to learn the name and the title of the person to whom your letter should be addressed. Most people, and that includes editors, are flattered by getting letters addressed personally, with their names spelled right and their titles correct, rather than by something of the "Dear Sir" or "Dear Editor" type. Most metropolitan newspapers have picture editors. If they haven't, write to the managing editor. Daily newspapers and the names of their principal editors are listed in the *Editor &*

Publisher Year Book. If your public library doesn't have a copy, try a local paper or advertising agency. Or you may be able to buy a copy from the Editor & Publisher Company, 1475 Broadway, New York 18. Of course, if you are in a big city, it will be easy to telephone the newspaper and ask the telephone operator for the name of the picture or managing editor.

I don't know whether Arnold Hardy, who was a Georgia Tech student at the time he came to photo fame, had made a previous canvass of the market for spot-news pictures. But his experience is graphic proof that the man on the spot can scoop the staff photographers of the major press associations and newspapers.

Hardy was around when the Winecoff Hotel in Atlanta, Georgia, burned in December, 1946. You should remember the dramatic photographs he made of bodies hurtling through the air as the trapped guests jumped to escape the licking flames. His pictures were given world-wide distribution by the Associated Press, which paid handsomely for his night's work.

However, whether it pays to follow Hardy's example and give all your photographs to one outfit is open to argument. That is why we advise thoroughly investigating all possible purchasers. If you make your survey in advance, then you will have some facts upon which to base a decision at the moment when spot-news luck comes your way.

For instance, contrasted with Hardy's market method is the more recent experience of Frank O. Seed of Niagara Falls, New York. Seed and his wife have run a fair-sized photographic operation in Niagara Falls for a long time. He is a thoroughly capable professional photographer. For years he has been the first cameraman on the scene when something happens at the Falls.

You must have seen the photographs of the helicopter rescue of a woman trapped in the rapids in May, 1950. All three major press associations had varying shots which they transmitted by wire. Yet all three got their pictures from Seed. Evidently on the basis of previous experience he decided that making enough negatives to give different views to all three agencies would produce a greater immediate money return and more good will all around for the future than the returns from an exclusive sale to a single outfit.

So when it comes to selling your news pictures, you must decide for yourself whether to try for a big price on an exclusive basis or whether to submit your pictures to a number of clients non-exclusively. Many of you will try first one method and then the other. After all that old trial-and-error method is the best teacher. However, you may be guided to a wise decision by the following outline of the situation:

Newspapers and press associations alike naturally prefer exclusive pictures. But none of them likes to be beaten on a big picture story. That means you can safely assume that none will insist on exclusivity of pictures or subject, if it means doing without pictures altogether. They will be happier if you have slightly different photographs to offer each, but in a pinch they will all use the same photograph if the story is important enough.

Years ago photographers often made a batch of prints from a single negative for submission to a dozen or more spots on a non-exclusive basis. But nowadays, as will be explained in a moment, it is an almost absolute requirement that you ship your clients undeveloped film. And if your story is big enough, every one of your potential customers will be seeking a selection of photographs, not just a single shot. So if you plan to offer your pictures to several possible clients and you want to give each a good selection, your best bet now is to make as many and as varied negatives as time and circumstances allow. In short, be ready to shoot your head off at the scene of any news break. Furthermore, don't stay at a fixed spot if there is opportunity to move around. The more varied camera angles you can get, the more usable photographs you will produce from a single spot-news story.

Now, for how to get your pictures to market. You should know that nowadays all important pictures are transmitted by wire and wireless. Only twenty years ago there was no wire-photo transmission; regularly scheduled airplane flights were infrequent and slow compared with those of today; even chartered planes and trains didn't approximate the present-day speed. So the lapse between the event and the time pictures of it could be received was often a matter of days and, from far-off places, even weeks and months. That meant pictures were fresh, and hence salable, for weeks. Today pictures are often stale and practically unsalable to press associations and newspapers even a few hours after an event.

Because wired delivery is so fast, the tempo of picture handling has been stepped up all along the line, right from the man who takes the picture. He may be you. That's why we stress preparedness for the day you make those historic photos. If you want to sell them, you must get them to market first. That, in most cases, means to the nearest point possessing facilities for transmitting photographs by wire. Hence it is essential that you know in advance the nearby sending points of the syndicate or syndicates with which you may wish to do business. Each press association will tell you where its closest transmitter is. In addition study the maps of the picture circuits of the three major agencies, so you will know other sending points in case you are away from home.

With the need for speed in mind, we offer some more pointers. The first is a general rule: Don't stop to develop your pictures of a spot-news event. There will be an occasional exception. In fact we will mention some later on. But most of the time it will pay you to follow that rule. Hardy, because he and the AP bureau were in the same town—Atlanta—made his own delivery to the office. But he lost precious time by doing his own processing. The excellence of his pictures, however, overcame the handicap of tardy delivery.

Many of you, especially the professionals with well-equipped darkrooms, may object to this. I can understand your feeling that no one will handle your precious films as carefully as yourself. That argument may have some merit in isolated instances. But remember that those on the receiving end, whether they are newspaper or press-association people, are just as anxious as you to get good, printable negatives. It is intelligent self-interest on their part to be extra careful when processing a contributor's film.

Furthermore, if you process your films yourself, you lose time all along the line in getting your pictures off to market. You must wait until the negatives are dry before you ship them; but drying time can be saved at their destination because it is possible to print enlargements from wet negatives. Also you may miss the best plane or train connections, permitting some competitor to get to market before you. Usually the first pictures received possess the greatest news value. That means they must be purchased without waiting to see what some tardier contributor may forward. Time, in most instances, is more important than picture quality, unless photographs are exceptionally good or exceptionally bad. Even when your pictures outclass the field, late arrival will cut their price, if it doesn't eliminate all chance of a sale.

Another caution: although on occasion wet negatives have been shipped successfully, don't you do it! There is not only the likelihood of delay; there is also considerable risk to it. I still remember an unfortunate experience that happened quite a few years ago. Somewhere in the West Indies there was a serious plane crash. There were several fatalities. Most noted of the survivors was Jose Iturbi, the pianist. Others were Jean Dalrymple, now a theatrical producer, and Gloria Hollister, a member of many Beebe expeditions and a capable photographer. Miss Hollister had checked with us before starting for South America and was prepared to airmail any news pictures made en route. She did just that with several of the plane crash.

But instead of airmailing undeveloped film, Miss Hollister had her precious pictures processed on the island. Then before they had been thoroughly dried, they were packed and shipped. I forget what was used to keep the negatives from sticking together. Whatever it was, it didn't work as intended, but stuck to the negatives. We soaked some of the stuff off the negatives, but some of it stuck or left smeared spots and scratches. I think we finally used one negative that was just passable. We were disappointed, because it was a good story. Miss Hollister didn't get much cash return for her effort.

Some other shipping rules have stood the test of time.

This is one of them: when you ship undeveloped film, be very certain that it is wrapped light-tight. A good way to insure that is to save the boxes and wrappings which the manufacturer uses.

Mark your container "undeveloped" legibly and on all sides, so that there will be no chance of anyone opening the package anywhere but in the darkroom.

When time for shipping connections is very tight and you are using cut film, you can dispatch it in holders, sending one or two to each of your customers. Don't overlook this bit of caution: make certain that every holder bears your name and address so that there will be no doubt about its being returned to you. However, if you have enough time, it is better to package your film and keep the holders.

With your films, enclose in the package or attach to it a complete caption describing the action and including names and places. Be sure that all persons shown in close-ups are properly identified. That means not only names, but such essentials as military, political, and professional titles, *e.g.* Brig. Gen. John Green of the Pennsylvania National Guard; Lt. Gov. Joseph Brown of Iowa; Lucy White, Sioux City schoolteacher, etc.

Check and double check the spelling of all names, including first names, surnames, and initials if any. Full names are always better than initials if available. Be certain of correct titles and their spelling. There can be hundreds of John Smiths. Anything that will separate your John Smith from his countless namesakes should be included as part of the identification in your picture caption. It is always best to type your captions, and that is especially true of names. If a typewriter isn't available and you must write them out in longhand, by all means print every name. Often a scribbled word can be made out from the context. But editors can't do that with proper names.

Normal identification of groups is from left to right. If you conform, say so, and if you are using some other system, make caption mention of it. (No editor will assume that you are using the left to right system unless you tell him so in your caption.)

Both on your caption sheet and directly on the box—or if there isn't room on the outside, then on a separate sheet inside the box—note the type of film used, exposure time, whether outdoors or indoors, and any other pertinent information that should prove helpful to the technician who processes your films.

It is often wise, unless time before plane, train, or bus departure is very short, to phone your editor and tell him what you have before sending off your shipment. It may be that he will not want your pictures, in which case you can immediately try offering them to other markets. On the other hand, if he does want them, he may have suggestions on routing that will save time. Also, if he wants the pictures at all, he will want to know how they are coming and when they are due, so that someone will be ready to receive them. If they are coming by air, he may want a motorcycle messenger to meet the plane and pick them up at the airport. He can also do several other things to expedite handling—for example notifying the laboratory so technicians will be waiting to develop the films, and alerting other editors so they will know when to schedule prints for the engraving room or the wires.

While we are talking about time and speed, we should get around to the minicams, those tiny, highly effective little cameras that use motion-picture film. Fine-grain developing produces negatives from which excellent enlargements for newspaper reproduction can be made. The camera's small size is also a great advantage in other ways. It is inconspicuous, permitting its use where other cameras might be barred or might make subjects self-conscious. Film for it costs less, and there is much less bulk to carry around.

On the debit side, minicam film usually requires longer processing time than larger negatives. Also because magnification is so much greater, printing takes longer. Special equipment helps overcome these difficulties, and most newspapers and press associations have everything needed to handle 35-millimeter film. But they can do a faster and often a much better job with larger negatives.

For these and other reasons, most press photographers use cameras handling 4 by 5 inch cut film. Hence newspaper laboratory equipment and technicians alike are geared to best results with that size. Next in order of preference are the 3¼ by 4¼ inch cut film, then the roll film, for 2¼ inch square exposures, used in the Rollei and other small reflex-type cameras. The Rolleis have some of the advantages of the minicams, without the handicap of the smallest-sized film. They still have the economy of smaller size; also, you are using less film, and rolls are cheaper than cut film. However, the whole roll must be developed even though you have only a single exposure. And if you are submitting your material undeveloped, you must send the whole roll to one place. The same number of exposures with cut film might permit submission to several publications.

Of course, if your story is hot enough, some of the usual rules can be disregarded. Take the case of Max Peter Haas, the lucky cameraman on the spot when two hold-up men trying to escape shot down a policeman on Fifth Avenue, New York. The episode happened around the corner from Haas's office, just as he stepped out of the building. Haas carries a Leica with him constantly, so he was prepared to catch the action. His outstanding pictures were splashed in the New York *News* the next morning.

As it happens, Haas broke almost all the rules we have been giving you. But his case is an exception because he had several advantages that most of us would lack. To start with, he is the head of an enterprising news picture service, European Photos, an outfit that can perhaps best be described if we copy baseball's gradings. As compared with the big three, we would call European an active AA minor-league club. Because Haas uses his Leica all the time, his laboratory was equipped for excellent handling of movie film. In his case self-processing of his films was no handicap, because his market was less than a mile away; developing time would have been the same at either place, and there were no transit connections to miss. Taxicabs are always available. And Haas really hit a jackpot. So far, total earnings of those pictures have topped $4,000.

A jackpot like this on a spot-news picture break is, as we said at the start, largely a matter of luck. However, we repeat, because too much emphasis cannot be put upon it, the admonition to take your camera with you all the time. Then you are always ready for a break.

Furthermore, you can even do something about being where a news break may occur. There isn't a photographic staff in the world big enough to cover every scheduled event. Even if there were, no one would wish to, for the chance of usable photographs would be too slim at the lesser events. But if you have the time, the uncovered spots are those to which you should go. It won't take much study of the newspapers in your territory to indicate which sports events, public meetings, and the like they cover photographically. In the large cities there are always several events scheduled for the same time, and some must necessarily go uncovered by the newspaper staff photographers. Nevertheless something unusual—for example, a bank of seats collapsing—can happen at a minor as well as at a major show. But there will be less chance of competition from staff photographers at the minor event. So study the habits of your local or nearby news photographers. Then pick the likeliest spots among those that they overlook. Station yourself there ready to act. Spot-news lightning can strike anywhere. But you can catch it only if you are prepared.

Fun and Profit in Features

THERE IS NO GAINSAYING the thrill of being on the spot for a major news event, getting the first pictures, and hitting the newspaper or syndicate jackpot for plenty of dough. But (and it is a very big but) the chances of doing that are slimmer than winning the Irish Sweepstakes or hitting a daily double at the race-tracks.

However, one phase of news photography allows the cameraman to call his own shots. In features he doesn't wait for things to happen. He goes out and finds or creates the situations or settings that provide the opportunity for photographs.

If the man with the camera has the proper type of pictorial vision and a sense of news value, making feature pictures for publication can be very profitable. Besides, it can be lots of fun. Feature photography is an art form in the truest sense of the words, and like any other art form, it is best when truly creative. The concept for a picture series must be born in the mind of the cameraman before it can be recorded on film. Few experiences can be more satisfying than starting out with an idea, carrying on through the shooting and processing of the photographs, gathering caption material, and finally seeing your baby blooming as a newspaper or magazine spread.

On the basis of this glowing picture of the fun in features, don't go overboard. Getting established as a free-lance in any field is a long and uphill struggle. It is especially tough in photography, where the competition is expert and keen. Go slowly and build up a reputation before you jump into the feature field with both feet. With the almost universal forty-hour work week, any job leaves plenty of time for the cameraman to pursue an avocation. Making photography for newspapers and magazines a sideline is much better than scrimping along trying to make it a full-time occupation. Then, too, if you must press, because that next acceptance and the accompanying check are so necessary, the spontaneity so important in feature pictures may very well disappear.

Before we get further into the subject, we should be agreed as to what we mean by feature photography. One definition is that features are not spot news. That is a negative approach, but a sound one. Another way is to define feature photography as telling a story with photographs and text. That's just the reverse of illustrating, where the story is told verbally and the pictures are the accompaniment. To tell a feature picture story may require only a single picture and a very few words. Or it may require dozens or even hundreds of photographs with text running to several thousand words. Subjects and circumstances will always be the determining factors.

Feature photography can be likened to a musical composition, with pictures taking the place of the solo and with words filling in the way an instrumental accompaniment does. And as in music the orchestral background is part of the composition, so also are words most necessary in feature pictures. They fill in with exact identifications of the people and places pictured. Sometimes they call attention to important details in the photographs. By and large, this verbal accompaniment is an important one in making feature pictures that will sell.

Almost every Sunday newspaper contains varied examples of feature photographs. So do magazines like *Life, Look,* the *Saturday Evening Post, Collier's,* and others. A study of them will show you how other photographers developed a story in a sequence of photographs.

The materials for feature pictures lie all about us. No one but you can see them for yourself. And if you can't visualize them first, you can't put them on to film for a feature series. Sometimes a feature idea may literally come up to your front porch. An example of that was played up in *Life* recently—a series of pictures showing wild animals feeding at night, used as a spread in that magazine on September 4, 1950. They were made by F. F. Stoody of Western Ways, Tucson, Arizona. He shot the pictures from the front window of his home in the foothills of the Tucson mountains. Besides the opportunity of having animals nearby, the main ingredients for Stoody's composition were the ability to realize the picture possibilities of such a situation and the patience to wait night after night for the right moment to shoot the pictures of the animals feeding in front of his house. It took restraint, too, not to rush the first few pictures to market. It was a matter of months before the collection was complete and ready to be submitted.

Usually making a feature photographic series requires more planning. This is the way it is done in the picture services:—the starting point is always an idea—sometimes from a cameraman, sometimes from an editor, sometimes from someone outside the photo department; the origin doesn't matter. The next step is to discuss it with editors and cameramen. Occasionally after thorough discussion, the original concept is modified or altogether discarded, for often, although the story is interesting, the editors cannot figure out how to tell it in a series of still pictures. Where motion is a governing factor, they have often passed up stories that might have produced swell movie features, but just wouldn't fit into still-picture molds. If the basic idea can survive those hurdles, then the editors are ready for the next step.

As the sequence idea develops, notes are made of the picture possibilities. From those notes a shooting script is drawn up for the guidance of the cameraman. There may be photographers who can produce excellent features "shooting off the cuff," but it is really not a sound practice. Ample preparation (so you know what you're after) and written notes (so you don't forget key shots) always pay off with better results. No matter how you do it, know in advance what you seek and how you want to develop your picture story.

When the shooting script is finished it ordinarily includes the minimum number of photographs needed, indicates which should be verticals and which horizontals, which close-ups and which long-shots, as well as the outline of the story, and the picture steps necessary to tell it. Then editors and cameramen go into a huddle over details, personally if the local staff is doing the job and by mail if the assignment is far away. As a creative feature photographer, most of the time you will have to be both editor and cameraman, at least until you submit your series for publication.

Remember, however, that the shooting script is a guide, not a rigid pattern into which every picture must fit like the pieces in a jigsaw puzzle. That is unnecessarily restrictive. The best method is to treat the shooting script as an outline which provides the basic design, but from which the cameraman is free to depart whenever he feels that by doing so he will produce better pictures.

Picture-service practice in general follows all these steps. However, there is wide variation in shooting scripts. Some are very complete; others are the barest of outlines. Every editor has his own methods, and often they vary to fit the temperaments of the cameramen assigned. Some need scripts with the most minute details. Others can develop outstanding series from the briefest oral descriptions of the pictures wanted. Though there is general agreement on well-thought-out preparation, the press of other duties, the timing of events that may fit into a feature sequence, and other factors often prescribe short cuts in writing shooting scripts. For instance, notes can be sketches as well as words. Use either or both, depending upon the story and your facility with words or drawing.

Obviously, when the cameraman is far away and has had little or no experience covering assignments for a picture service, the use of a well-planned script is indicated. From Metro Service comes an example of such a script. It resulted in a set of eleven pictures distributed for publication on Sunday, August 21, 1949, and used in lay-outs by nine of the Metro Roto sections on that or a succeeding date. It reads:

SHOOTING SCRIPT

NOTE: These pictures must appear as unposed as possible. We would like to have them look as if they had been clipped from a Pete Smith Short.

THE HOME IS A DANGEROUS PLACE

CHARACTERS: Dave O'Brien
Dorothy O'Brien
Neighbor's child

1. Scene: kitchen. Semi-close-up of Dave sitting on the floor with a dazed expression on his face. Broken dishes on and around him point to the fact that he was helping his wife with the dinner dishes when he slipped and fell. The cause of his accident is seen in the immediate foreground—a roller skate.
2. Mrs. O'Brien has rushed down to the kitchen, while getting dressed, to make sure that the dinner is progressing as it should. We see her in a semi-distant shot as she half turns toward the camera to plug in some electrical appliance. Unhappily, Mrs. O'Brien is dressed in the frilliest housecoat possible. One of the ruffles of this creation has caught on the handle of a pot full of hot fat to be used in frying chicken. When she moves again, Dorothy is going to be a very unhappy woman. Note: Make pot handle caught by ruffle a center of interest.
3. Dave is very handy around the house. We see him in semi-close-up as he teeters on top of the small boxes placed on a chair to enable him to reach the ceiling light he was fixing. Dave is going to land on a stove busily cooking the O'Brien dinner.
4. Close-up of Dave as he sleepily reaches into the medicine cabinet without trying to see what it is he is reaching for. He thinks it's Bromo-Seltzer. Unfortunately, it is a bottle of poison exactly the same shape and size as the Bromo-Seltzer bottle beside it.
5. Extreme close-up of Dave's leg as it reaches out of the bathtub to find footing on the wet bathroom floor. Dave doesn't know it but he is about to step on the cake of soap which he dropped and didn't bother to pick up.
6. With the top of the kitchen stove in the immediate foreground, shoot beyond at Dave sitting at the kitchen table. He has come downstairs to make himself a midnight snack, the ingredients of which are spread before him. While waiting for the coffee to boil, he has fallen asleep and

doesn't know that the pot has boiled over, putting out the flame but not the gas.

7. Semi-close-up of Dave hanging by his middle from the branch of a tree in the O'Brien yard. His ragged clothes and blackened face show that he has recently been in an explosion. The latter was caused by the cleaning fluid which he was using on the pants still held in one limp hand. Miraculously, the pants are still unscathed. Shoot up at him.
8. Semi-close-up of Dave caught half-way in his descent to the floor in the chair he was tilting. He is waving arms and legs, madly trying to save himself from the bad fall he is going to have. His newspaper floats in the air above him.
9. Close-up of Dave nicely asleep in his bed. The light is still on and the book on his chest tells us that he has fallen asleep while reading. The smoke curling up around him also tells us that he has fallen asleep with a lighted cigarette in his hand. If Brunhilde O'Brien doesn't wake up soon, he will be on his way to Valhalla.
10. Dave is going hunting and busily cleans the gun in his lap, meanwhile boasting to Dorothy of former hunting exploits. Neither of them notices that the gun is pointed directly at her. Dave hasn't checked to see whether or not it is loaded.
11. Extreme close-up of a brat (the next door neighbor's) who has happily wandered into the O'Brien kitchen and discovered a lovely box of matches. Some of the matches are scattered about him and he is about to scratch a chubby fistful on the sandpaper strip of the box in his hand.
12. Shooting up from a highly waxed floor with its pretty little islands of scatter rugs, the camera catches Dave O'Brien entering the room with a tray full of refreshments. It would be nice, if possible, if we could catch Dave as he starts to skate down the room on one of these little rugs.
13. Close-up, shooting down, at Dave happily soaking in the tub. He is reaching out to tune the small radio teetering on the edge of the tub. He has never heard that electrical equipment and water are bad companions. The radio in the water, since he will upset it, is going to do every bit as good a job as the Sing Sing chair.

No matter what sort of script he uses, the cameraman who makes the photographs has the ultimate responsibility for producing a publishable set of pictures. His vision and his knowledge of his instrument—the camera—produce the pictorial compositions with story-telling impact. If he can't get the idea through his lens and onto film, all the advance planning and shooting scripts are worthless.

And this brings us right back to you. You must have a feeling for feature pictures if you hope to produce marketable sequences. You can decide whether you possess or lack the spark for yourself, or you can choose the more expensive method of letting editors do it by constantly rejecting your offerings.

While we're still on the subject of shooting scripts, we might add that upon occasion you may find it pays to throw the script away. The cameraman arriving at the scene of his story may find circumstances radically different from the concept upon which the shooting script was based. Faced with such a situation, the photographer lacking imagination or slavishly following instructions may return to his office without a picture, while a keener man may come back with a picture story far better than the one he was originally assigned.

A little incident that happened some years ago illustrates that perfectly. The New York office of one of the major picture organizations wrote to its London office asking that a photographer be sent to Somersby, Lincolnshire, to make a series of pictures on the original of Tennyson's Brook—the one which "runs on forever." The photographer was duly dispatched, but no photographs reached New York. So a query was sent, which brought the reply that when the cameraman arrived at the village of Somersby, the brook was dry. Far from running on forever, it had not the tiniest trickle of water in it. So the photographer never opened his camera. Had he used his imagination, he would have realized that pictures of that brook gone dry would have had more news feature value than those of it full of water. But by the time the report got to New York it was too late to do anything about it.

As the editor who made the original assignment and then called London's attention to missing a better story, we are still puzzled that experienced editors, as well as the photographer, muffed so obvious a picture story.

At this point it would be a good idea to remind you of the necessity for variety in the shape of your photographs. Depending upon your equipment, your choice is limited to either square negatives or oblongs. Obviously if your camera uses square film, the only way you can vary shapes is by leaving air on the film and cropping when you make enlargements, so that resulting pictures may be either squares, horizontals, or verticals. Where oblong film is used, turning the camera will produce either verticals or horizontals right on the negative.

There is a good reason for this reminder about shapes. Taking advantage of opportunities for variety will help you sell your pictures. Quite often subject matter governs the position of the camera and the shape of the resulting pictures. Obviously, making a photograph of a tall building means holding the camera vertically. General views of events, whether civic or sports, usually call for horizontal shots. But most of the time the cameraman has a choice; and much too often he doesn't exercise it. Take a second shot of the same subject so you can submit one horizontal and one vertical. This gives an editor the choice of a picture that will best fit his make-up needs, and makes it that much easier to sell a picture. This is more important in feature pictures than in spot-news coverage, though it helps there too.

For making feature photographs, not only is it necessary to tell a story, but the individual prints must possess enough variety in subject matter, composition, and shape to fit into a pleasing lay-out, either on a single page or on a series of pages. Page sizes are rigidly fixed. So editors and artists use devices like bleeding pictures over the edge of the page and cropping into squares, oblongs, ovals, circles, and other shapes to get variety. The effort is both to avoid monotony and to present each picture most effectively. Naturally if all your pictures are the same shape the make-up men's task in fitting them into good lay-outs will be more difficult and on occasion well-nigh impossible. And when you get action or other subject matter right up to the edge of your negative or print, you complicate the task all the more. Sometimes to meet lay-out requirements, sky or foreground have been painted into pictures, but it would have been much better for the photographer to have put them into his picture in the first place.

Most cameramen don't realize it, but the photographer who makes a picture for publication is the first in the series of persons who will edit the picture. When he looks through his finder or ground glass and decides how much will be recorded on his film he is to an extent editing the picture. He sets the limits for all the others. They can subtract from that, but they cannot add.

Realizing that, photographers should use restraint in editing their negatives. There will be occasions when the biggest close-up filling all your negative is desirable. But most of the time you will be better off if you leave a little air around the edges of your pictures. That means on the sides as well as at the top and bottom. And it applies both to the original exposure and to printing enlargements from negatives. It also applies if you work with color instead of black and white, except that here there is no control after the original exposure, as there is in making enlarged prints in black and white.

That doesn't mean that you should carry this advice out to absurdity by covering so much ground that important details wind up as pinpoints on your negatives. Nor does it mean entire negatives should be enlarged without some cropping to emphasize the heart of your picture. But it does most definitely mean that you shouldn't overdo things by trying to make prints that leave editors no choice except to use them as they are or reject them entirely. That is very bad salesmanship.

The ultimate shape of your pictures as they are published rests with the editor-artist team that lays out the pages. If they can't make your pictures fit their pages, they won't buy them from you.

Before we wind up this discussion of how to make feature pictures, here are some practical hints that apply to all feature-picture coverage. Because there is always a considerable time lapse between the shooting and the publication of feature layouts, the cameraman must be watchful to avoid backgrounds that will too definitely date his pictures. For example, if there is snow on the ground, the picture series must be rushed for publication before the winter is over or be held dormant for almost a year.

And that can be bad, because buildings, roads, and other physical aspects of a site may be changed in that time.

If, for instance, you are planning a picture story for summer publication, be sure that any outdoor shots show green grass and leaves on the trees. If the pictures are to be used in spring and fall, don't have midsummer foliage in your backgrounds. The position of the sun and the length of shadows are also clues to the seasons. Watch them when you are working on a set to be used far in the future.

Take care about the way people dress. Overcoats are definitely out of place in summer pictures, just as shirt-sleeves would be for outdoor shots up north in wintertime. Try to avoid extreme styles that may go out of fashion before your pictures reach publication. And be on the watch for local lags in keeping up with styles. Unless your pictures are telling the story of the locality's dress idiosyncrasies, don't photograph teen-agers wearing long skirts when all over the country short skirts are in style.

Sometimes making pictures one year and holding them for use the next is not only justified but absolutely necessary. Magazines particularly work months ahead and therefore must often make pictures when they are seasonable and then wait until that season rolls round again before publishing them. That is particularly true of observances of Christmas, Easter, and other major holidays. There is nothing wrong with that, just as long as everybody concerned is honest about it. It is common practice to photograph Easter Dawn services and other special observances, not for the next day's publication but the next year's.

But whenever you make your pictures, be sure to tell the editors when and where, without quibbling. Exact dates are best. They may not show up in the final cut-lines but they are very valuable as guidance to the editors who use your pictures. And when you submit year-old pictures, call attention to any changes you may know about. If some of the participants, especially those having leading roles in an Easter Passion Play, for example, have died or are being replaced for other reasons, tell the editor. Usually it will not make any difference, but let him be the judge of that. And he will like you better, because he will know that you can be trusted.

To stay in business and progress as a feature photographer, you must do more than convince editors that you know how to make acceptable pictures and have good story ideas. You must prove trustworthy. Always be sure that your pictures and your captions are telling the truth, not concealing it. No editor can go out into the field to check what you picture or what you say about your pictures. He must take you on faith, so good faith and truthfulness are important ingredients in building up acceptance for your contributions.

Unless you can sell them, making feature pictures will produce neither profit nor much fun. Individual markets for each type of news picture will be treated fully in the proper chapters. But it is fitting here to outline the general markets for feature material, with some hints as to selling procedure. There are several ways of selling, either direct or through an agent. No one can tell you which is best for you. Consider them all and then choose what you prefer.

The greatest cash returns for picture sets will come from the enormous-circulation, slick-paper national magazines. As a rule the top prices are paid by *Life, Saturday Evening Post, Collier's, Holiday,* and the other leaders. Naturally for this reason the competition is keener, a fact which raises the odds against your making a sale. If you watch these publications carefully, you will also notice that, with minor exceptions, most of the picture sets are produced by regulars whose work appears rather steadily. For the most part they are full-time staffers or free-lances who for all practical purposes are almost on a staff basis.

Next in line as good paying possibilities are the rotogravure and magazine sections of the leading metropolitan newspapers. Many of them pay exceedingly well for color and black and white. In this category are the New York *News* Roto, the New York *Times* Sunday Magazine Section, the *Sunday Mirror* Magazine, Pictures of the St. Louis *Post-Dispatch,* and many others. We might also include syndicated Sunday sections like *This Week* and *Parade.* There are also a few house organs circulated widely to consumers that are in the market for feature picture series. They also pay well.

Next in descending order as to prices paid, but probably at

the top in ratio of acceptances, are the picture services. They are in the market for picture series—usually rather short—for distribution to members or subscribers, and in some instances for sale to other publications. Among them are Acme Roto Service, International News Photos By-Line Features, the Metropolitan Group, and Wide World Photos. They don't pay very much in comparison with the slick magazines, but some of them over the course of a year buy a great many pictures. As in all submissions of pictures for publication, an element of luck is involved in feature sales. A lot depends upon *when* your material hits them. If their own staff photographers are in high production on feature pictures, they will be buying less from contributors.

Last of all you can turn your material over to an agent to sell for you. There are several of these in New York City and a few elsewhere. Several agencies are quite large; others are practically one-man outfits. Basically they act as your salesman and for that service take 50 percent of the gross proceeds of each sale as their commission. Their advantage is closeness to and acquaintance with the principal customers, which permits offering your pictures all around much faster than can be done directly by mail. They can save you time and money in correspondence and in making prints. There are advantages and disadvantages which will be gone into fully in the chapter on picture services. You don't need an agent if you have the time and inclination to handle correspondence and other selling chores yourself.

Whether you deal directly or through an agent, it usually pays to query publications before you start shooting a feature series. Until you have established a reputation for performance you cannot expect to get an overnight order on an inquiry backed up with nothing but an outline of the proposed picture series. But you may get an expression of interest and an invitation to submit your pictures. Or (and this can be equally helpful in keeping you from aiming at an impossible target) you may receive definite word that the publication is not at all interested in your picture story. Often, too, if a publication expresses interest, the editor will include suggestions as to how to make your pictures more acceptable to his book.

Most publications prefer that you query before sending pictures, even if your set is completed. Usually you can tell an editor enough in a brief letter to permit him to decide whether your material is not for him or whether it has enough possibilities to warrant your forwarding negatives or prints.

Perhaps it will be profitable now to look into the methods of some photographers who have done rather well in producing and marketing feature photographs. Our first example is Charles J. Herbert, who started as a free-lance movie cameraman in Florida and now operates Western Ways Photographic Services in Tucson, Arizona. A full-time feature-picture business, Western Ways is an apparent exception to our rule that all news photography, and that includes feature photography, is not to be recommended as a good living. Actually it is no exception. Its commercial, studio, and photo-finishing phases have made up any losses from its feature operations. Western Ways' story is an interesting one, and it will give an aspiring free-lance an idea of the difficulties, expenses, and hard work involved in setting up this type of photo business.

When he started in Tucson, Herbert had already won wide recognition as a newsreel feature cameraman. He and his wife, Lucile, had made some still pictures while making newsreels, but they were not well known in the still field. Though they set up shop in Tucson about ten years ago, they really didn't get going until Herbert came back from overseas service in World War II.

The Herberts started Western Ways with a backlog of 35-millimeter movie film and a few still negatives. They began by setting up Western Ways to produce and market feature-picture stories. Herbert still considers that to be the service's principal occupation and devotes most of his own time to it. Studio, commercial, and photo-finishing departments came later. Though profitable, Herbert looks upon them as sidelines. He prefers to make feature-picture scenes or to help cameramen and writers produce them. Occasionally in emergencies he will cover spot news, but he has no liking for it.

The Herberts' principal profit, aside from drawing some business to other departments, has been the satisfaction of doing something they enjoy. As they put it: "While the venture has not paid off in cash dividends, it has spread the fame of the West and its people to more and more places in our land and throughout the world—and it has sent many writers and photographers along their way with more know-how and success to their credit and it has built the finest and most extensive documentary file of the Rocky Mountain area." For from that tiny collection of 35-millimeter film and a modest number of stills with which the Herberts started, the Western Ways library has grown to approximately 30,000 black-and-white negatives and 6,000 color transparencies.

Because Tucson is so far away from the major publishing centers, Western Ways, like the individual free-lance, must use the mails for marketing. That is why a study of their operation is such a good guide to anyone trying to sell his own photographic product.

From the first the Herberts decided they would aim for more than just the top markets. Material is sent everywhere, right down to the smallest trade papers, which pay very small sums for photographs. Of course when exclusivity is one of the marketable items, the first offerings are made to the publications paying top prices. Then, until a sale is made, a set of pictures is kept shuttling back and forth to publications lower down on the list. Few of their photos fail to land some place. Western Ways never sets a price when offering picture stories. All submissions are made at the going rates of the publications. Often, after accepting several Western Ways offerings, both large and small publications increase the prices paid.

We asked the Herberts to pick an outstanding example of their picture-story coverage. They selected their assignment to photograph Dr. Lytle S. Adams applying his method of reseeding the Arizona desert to grass. His technique was to drop from airplanes pellets containing seed, fertilizer, rodent repellant, and a mud covering to keep birds from eating the seeds. Western Ways, covering from the air and on the ground, told the story fully with pictures and text. National magazine and Sunday rotogravure-section acceptance was very high. Total sales ran over $3,000 and the end is not yet in sight. Recently there has been a renewed flurry of orders from England for both pictures and text.

Western Ways' method of dividing sales proceeds may provide a guide to equitable sharing. Here's how it's done:

When it is finally decided to go ahead on a feature-picture story, and locations, shooting script, and other details have been worked out, the company supplies film, bulbs, and other materials, and pays traveling expenses, etc. All that is charged against the assignment. When the project is completed and the first sale is made, Western Ways is reimbursed for those costs before there is any division of proceeds. If the cameraman worked alone, he gets 50 percent of the total after expenses. Western Ways retains the other 50 percent. If a writer was a member of the team there is a three-way split, with each participant—cameraman, writer, and Western Ways—being credited with 33⅓ percent.

Western Ways has a tenet that is a good one for all photographers. The Herberts do not let publicity creep into their feature-picture assignments. They do not distribute publicity pictures gratis nor do they accept fees to include publicity pictures in their feature lay-outs. The commercial department will cover such assignments for anyone paying for that service, but coverage is all it will do. The client does his own distributing. However, if a commercial assignment has the germ of a feature story, Western Ways will try to work it up, but strictly as a story and without a publicity tie-in.

It takes time to build up any business. Western Ways is finally achieving a cumulative marketing effect that hit-or-miss operations would never bring. It now gets many calls for pictures from files and an increasing number of assignments for stories in its territory. But this also entails payroll, office, and library expenses that amount to a pretty penny. And I am sure the Herberts will agree that their operation is really hard work. Obviously, the number of photographers who have the financial resources, the stamina, and the ability to achieve success in so highly competitive a field is very limited.

There is undoubtedly more fun and possibly more net profit in making feature photography an avocation. Thus Charles J.

Belden made photography pay profits, but in the thirty years he lived at Pitchfork, Wyoming, it was not his principal means of livelihood. His main business was ranching. Photography with both still and movie cameras was his fun. It also provided the excuse for occasional trips East to call upon editors and sell pictures which more than paid the cost of the trips. As a matter of fact, in those days we used to look forward to having him drop in with collections of Rocky Mountain pictures.

Though he moved to St. Petersburg, Florida, about eight years ago, Belden is still selling Wyoming pictures. Only recently he received an order for a print of a picture originally published in a 1925 issue of the *National Geographic Magazine.* His Wyoming pictures prove the point that opportunities for feature photographs lie all about. Belden pictured his region, scenery, livestock, wild animals, and friends and neighbors. And because they were good pictures and told a story, he sold them. He preferred personal calls, but when we asked him whether he would have done as well submitting by mail, he confessed he wasn't certain. The determining factor in his case was the opportunity to come East, meet old friends, and keep personal contacts.

We asked Belden, too, which of his pictures brought in the best cash return. His reply was a surprise because it seems we had a part, though a rather minor one, in the series of events that saved the negative for him. Here's Belden's story.

It was very cold in Pitchfork one January 13th in the thirties. The Beldens were sitting close to the fire, listening to the radio, when the telephone rang at 11 P.M. The New York office of Paramount News was calling. There had been a plane crash at Miles City, Montana, about three hundred miles away. They wanted Belden to start for the scene immediately. He threw movie and still picture gear into his car and was on his way.

By chance there was a partly exposed roll of still film in Belden's camera. When he got to the scene he shot a newsreel for Paramount and then used the remaining still exposures to make shots for us at Times Wide World Photos. The roll reached New York undeveloped and when Wide World Photos processed the film we found not only good wreck shots which were used but several uncaptioned scenics. Those were immediately returned to Belden.

One of them was a horse picture, which he has since sold between fifty and sixty times. That, he says, includes a sale to the New York *Times*. Once the shot was blown up to a mural 10 by 18 feet. All told, that negative, that only by chance got back to Pitchfork, has brought in over $3,000.

Getting away from reminiscence, Belden reported a recent discovery that may help all cameramen who have run into difficulty getting strangers to pose for them. He and his wife spent five months in 1950 making still pictures in Austria, Italy, Switzerland, and France. They accompanied Andre LaVarre, who was making movie shots.

Everywhere they went natives were reluctant to pose. They knew all about photographers who took up their time and promised to send them prints which they never received. But Belden was prepared. He had taken along a Polaroid Land camera and fifty rolls of eight-exposure film. The first step was to make an exposure and almost immediately present the subject with the finished photographs. That overcame all objections to performing for Belden's other cameras. Of course Belden brought back only five of those four hundred Polaroid shots.

Here is another tip from Belden's experiences. He reports that credit lines have a cash as well as a morale value. Quite often he submits his pictures first to magazines which pay smaller fees but print his credit line under his photos instead of hidden away in a box in the back of the book. He has found that reorders from persons who read the magazine and notice he took the pictures more than make up the difference in the price paid by the biggest publication.

Now for a newcomer in the feature field, young Marvin Goldman of Philadelphia. His approach is different in that he is using the camera as an art tool in place of brush, paint, and canvas. Besides, he is starting from scratch to make feature and artistic photography a gainful full-time occupation. How well he will make out only the future can tell, but his own account of how he made The Man in the Box series that *Life* used for Speaking of Pictures (September 18, 1950) should interest everyone who wants to produce feature-picture stories.

According to this graduate (June, 1950) of the Philadelphia Museum School of Art:

"The Man in the Box is one of five stories that I have presented using photography as my medium of expression. In creating The Man in the Box, as I have tried to do in my other stories, I first conceived the plot and mood of the story in my mind and then made hundreds of sketches, so that when the time came to photograph the story I would know exactly what I did and did not want (note: Goldman uses only sketches, no words). Naturally, while photographing, spontaneous situations always occur, and I tried to take advantage of them as best I could. The same thing applies in painting, and sometimes can be an important factor in the final result.

"The story cannot be told in words because the entire conception is based on still pantomime employing the use of realistic abstract shapes that work with the human figure to establish mood as desired. The reason for selecting the white box (cardboard carton painted a dull white) and the black umbrella was to push even further the contrast (size, shape, color) in the character of the man. He is a strange individual, and the use of the top hat is to make the observer realize still further the difference from the everyday man on the street.

"He likes to get away from the rest of the world, and do as he pleases, living in a world of his own (the box).

"Few people could appreciate my stories; some thought they were very bad, some liked them very much. I feel some encouragement because of the difference of opinion that people feel in my work. As long as it is not in between I am satisfied."

Goldman reports that photographing The Man in the Box took two hours. Including planning, sketching, processing, and printing, the project occupied two full days. *Life* paid him $250 for the lay-out. They used only seven of the fifty-five prints he submitted. He actually made almost eighty exposures. All his negatives are square, 2¼ by 2¼. The camera used was a Ciro-flex, the first outfit Goldman ever owned. The film was 120 Super XX and all the lighting was natural outdoors. Goldman made his sale through a personal call at the *Life* offices in New York. Since then he has received some assignments from other publications, but doesn't know whether the *Life* lay-out led to them.

This story is interesting not only because Goldman is fighting long odds in a toughly competitive field, but because he is trying at the same time a neat balancing trick. Along with his photography, he is trying to express himself in other art forms. He has been advised by experts that he should make up his mind to channel his talents either to painting or photography, if he wants a real chance for success.

Going Up in the Air for Pictures

SOONER OR LATER EVERY photographer goes up in the air. We mean that literally. After trying shots from ground level, he gets the urge for elevation. Usually he starts with chairs, then ladders, progressing to vantage points in high buildings, hilltops, fire towers, tops of silos—whatever is available in his vicinity.

Finally comes the impulse to see what can be shot from a plane. Quite often the first aerial pictures are not the result of previous planning. A chance opportunity for a flight, or a news assignment that cannot be covered satisfactorily except from directly overhead, may provide the opportunity.

While more pictures now are being taken from the air, the market for air shots made by free-lances seems to be shrinking. In the early days when airplanes were fewer and flights less frequent, taking air shots on speculation was often quite profitable. Their novelty lent news value, and mere novelty is something which aerial views no longer possess. To sell now, such pictures must have both pictorial and news impact. So if you must hire a plane to get them, we don't recommend making air views on speculation.

Photographs taken from airplanes do have many advantages in certain circumstances. Nothing can surpass the shots from a plane for effectiveness in making general views of wide-spread fires (either flaming city buildings or forest conflagrations), of train wrecks, plane wrecks (especially those in isolated areas), and of hurricane and tornado damage. Sea-disaster pictures are almost always air views nowadays, but they are generally made by Coast Guard or Navy photographers. Terrain, extent of the damage, and other factors will help the cameraman determine whether the most effective shots can be made from the air or the ground. No one can tell him in advance what to do under such circumstances. He must be there to see for himself.

Now you may wonder why, if speculative hiring of a plane is discouraged, space is being devoted here to a discussion of making aerial photographs. Actually there are many good reasons why such discussion can prove profitable. For one thing almost everybody flies these days in scheduled airliners or other planes for pleasure and business. And the fan who takes his camera along often can get pictures that are salable.

For another, the local photographer who has contributed to publications and picture services and has thereby established himself as a stringer correspondent to be called upon when news pictures are needed from his territory never knows when an assignment will come along that must be shot from the air. So he should know how to work from a plane. That's part of the basic concept that the cameraman who makes his plans and contacts well ahead of time will profit most when news breaks near him.

The private pilot is still another who should be prepared to market his pictures. Flying to and from work or just for pleasure, he should always have his loaded camera with him, ready to take advantage of picture opportunities. Even the professional aerial map makers would do well to consider opportunities for obliques and possible extra cash to be picked up as result of map-making flights. The old-timers did that all the time. There is no reason for not doing it now.

For the photographer who is thoroughly familiar with the instrument of his trade or hobby, making good aerials is not too difficult. However, a few pointers from professionals who have made it their livelihood should help to a good start. We have checked with several, asking the questions most cameramen would want answered. Among those questioned were news staffers who normally work on the ground but have flown many times, as well as specialists in aerial photography.

We'll start with the tips from one newsman, Carl D. Nesensohn, of Wide World Photos. His suggestions are simple and very practical. We can't recall whether he has ever used specially designed aerial cameras. We do know that he has made good air shots with the same cameras he used for day-in and day-out ground assignments. But let him speak for himself:

"If you should be working from a small plane, such as a Piper, Aeronca, or Luscombe, pick a still day for smooth air. Keep your shutter speed around 200 for shots of the ground at altitudes of from 300 to 400 feet. For air to air shots, such as planes in formation, you can run as slow as 100 in smooth air. For such shots, especially for cloud formations, use a filter. I suggest a K2 or a minus blue.

"Almost any camera will do for aerial shots of a news or semi-news nature. In a small plane the smaller the camera the better off you will be. No matter what the size of the camera, be sure to keep arms and elbows from contact with the plane. Otherwise the vibration of the craft will be transmitted through them to the camera. That will produce movement of your camera that will show up in your negatives. Kept away from direct contact with the body of the plane, the arms act as a shock absorber for the camera.

"Though I started with a tip about shots from 300 feet or so, that is much too low for flying over populated areas. If you fly your own ship, you will know the CAB regulations. If not, the pilot will know and will keep his craft at proper height. The longer the lens on your camera, the higher up you can stay, though not without losing some detail and speed. In many small planes the pilot can cut his engine and glide in over your picture target. The advantage is slower plane speed, which permits slower shutter speeds and the elimination of most of the craft's vibration."

Of course, Nesensohn's observations, especially the one about calm days, mostly apply when the photographer can choose his time for picture making. Many times on news assignments Nesensohn had to make his pictures on days that were far from calm. The news, unfortunately, will not wait upon the weather. But on feature jobs or when shooting to make scenics, the cameraman can usually wait until sun, wind, and clouds are just right for getting most effective pictures.

Nevertheless every aerial picture jaunt won't fit into your preconceived notions. Of course, you should know what you want to get. But don't set camera and expect to shoot away without adjustment. Circumstances, the nature of the picture objective, and other factors should govern shutter speed, lens openings, and the like. For example, one of the pictures that Nesensohn has treasured for years shows a cloud formation made from above at 15,000 feet. He was returning from Chicago to New York in an Army ship, long before the Air Force became a separate unit. The plane was a Lockheed Lodestar twin-engine job and it was very early in the morning, so the light was very poor. Though air specialists, like Robert Smith of Fairchild Aerial Surveys and Charles McLaughlin, frown upon shooting so slow, Carl made his cloud shots with a shutter speed of 1/10th of a second. The lens opening was set at *f/5.6.*

Now let us listen to the men who have specialized in making aerial photographs for news and commercial purposes. Most of these men have done much mapping too, but we shan't discuss this work for it is a separate field with little application to the making and selling of news pictures. We'll first turn to Charles McLaughlin. His experience goes back to the Curtiss Flying Service. Later he operated an aerial photographic outfit under his own name. Other interests keep him on the ground now, but he hasn't forgotten how to make air views.

According to McLaughlin, except for specific assignments, there is no money in making aerial news shots now. It is no longer, he says, a full-time business. That's why he got out. Mapping furnishes the bread and butter for the professional aerial cameraman these days. But up to the second world war McLaughlin found flying on news assignments not only profitable but a great deal of fun.

In an expansive mood McLaughlin recounted some of his exploits. You'll not only enjoy hearing them, but in each there is some lesson that can be applied when attempts at air views get you into similar spots.

One of his experiences proves that imagination and a keen eye can create a salable news picture literally out of the air. Some fifteen years ago Charley was making air maps of Gogebic County on the northern peninsula of Michigan. The terrain below was dotted with lakes, one of which was shaped like a

Gibson girl—or at least it appeared so to him. Accordingly, McLaughlin asked the pilot to drop down and come over that lake again so he could make an oblique shot.

This is as good a place as any to point out that in making news pictures and scenics from a plane, don't shoot straight down. Hold your camera at an angle of approximately 45 degrees to the land below. Straight-down verticals produce a flat picture, all right for maps, but rarely effective for pictorial purposes.

To finish Charley's story, he shot his lake, wrote a caption describing its resemblance to the figure of a Gibson girl, and when he got back to New York printed the film. With that caption he sold the Gibson girl lake both to the rotogravure section of the New York *Times* and to Wide World Photos. Thus he got extra profit from what started out as a routine mapping job.

On another occasion imagination and pictorial sense paid off even more profitably. McLaughlin and his pilot were deadheading back to New York from a fruitless mapping trip over Connecticut. Low clouds had prevented flying at the proper mapping altitude. So up to this point the trip had been a complete washout. As they approached Manhattan Island from the northeast at about 8,500 feet, McLaughlin caught a glimpse of the skyscrapers through the clouds.

So he started shooting. The resulting pictures were wonderful. He took them around himself and sold prints to both the *Times* and the *Herald Tribune* in New York for their rotogravure sections. Besides that, Times Wide World Photos distributed them widely. And made up into a three-panel screen, one of the shots won first prize at a *U.S. Camera* show. When the returns were all in, McLaughlin found the gross receipts were five times the amount the mapping job would have brought. And as a plus he got a blanket order from the Texas Oil Company to make more cloud pictures from the air.

Now here is a worthwhile tip from McLaughlin for those traveling on regularly scheduled airliners. In fact, it applies to some extent to any flying you may do. Always keep your camera handy, he advises. Plane windows are good spots from which to shoot pictures. But don't wait until you are almost on top of the scene you want. Start shooting as you approach and keep shooting until you pass the objective. In that way, says McLaughlin, the subject will loom up larger on your film as you get closer, with the very last shot often proving to be the best. Though it uses up your film a bit faster, multiplicity of shots usually pays off in better pictures. On the other hand, in a fast-moving plane waiting for a single shot may make you lose it altogether.

Here is another tip illustrated with a story from one of McLaughlin's news-assignment flights. Charley had been hired to make air views of the rowing regatta at Poughkeepsie. When he got over the Hudson River at regatta time he found the air full of planes with photographers on the same mission. All of them, of course, made many preliminary views, but the big picture would be the air shot at the finish.

Just as he would on a ground assignment, the air photographer, when he finds competition, looks for that different angle. So McLaughlin studied the river. He noticed that there was enough wind to produce a slight ripple on the surface of the stream. So right there he broke the rule that says news shots from the air should be obliques, not verticals. He decided conditions would favor a vertical.

As the shells hit the finish line, his plane was directly overhead. He pointed his camera straight down and shot. The resulting picture made the frail racing shells skimming the rippling Hudson look like "skippers," those tiny insects that seem to run on the surface of fresh water ponds. Again imagination and judgment produced an outstanding picture on a very competitive assignment.

While we're on the subject of breaking rules, we'll cite another McLaughlin experience where that paid off. Aerial photography has an old and fairly rigid rule about shots of buildings: *i.e.* sunlight should hit two sides of the structure for best results. And aerial photographers are advised against shooting directly into the sun. Mac broke both those precepts late one afternoon. His plane was over the Queensboro Bridge, which links Manhattan with Long Island. The sun was low, backlighting the tall buildings of the New York skyline. So he pointed his camera right at the sun and shot away.

His picture was widely used at the time, and it is still selling. He can't remember how much money it earned, but of the more than 50,000 aerial pictures he has made, the number of that negative is the only one he remembers. In his files it is #4,347.

At the start of this book we emphasized that being prepared for lucky news breaks pays off. We said that knowing where and how to market your pictures is something to learn before, not after, you make news pictures. Another McLaughlin experience proves that you can run into lucky news breaks in the air as well as on the ground.

Since he had been selling pictures for a long time, he had contacts with both picture services and newspapers, so he was prepared with marketing knowledge, though the rest of this episode was luck. McLaughlin had started out on a mapping job to photograph New York City's West Side Highway. The pilot started to circle around preparatory to leveling off at 12,500 feet for the mapping run. Just then McLaughlin saw a puff of smoke rise out of New York Bay. An instant later they would have been fully turned and not seen it.

The pilot, Gil Waller, shouted: "That's an explosion." "Forget it," replied Mac, "someone's stoking a furnace." "A helluva furnace," was Gil's comment as he raced the airplane toward the smoke.

He was right. The German steamer *Muenchen* had blown up in New York Harbor. Almost instantly on the scene, owing to the lucky break, McLaughlin shot a dozen pictures and flew back to his base, Curtiss Field, at Valley Stream, Long Island. Into the laboratory he rushed, cut off the exposed section of film in the darkroom, left it to be processed, and flew back to his mapping assignment.

When the fire scenes had been developed, the negatives were rushed to Times Wide World Photos in New York City. That gave that outfit pictures before cameramen alerted after the explosion could reach the scene by plane or boat. And other advance arrangements freed McLaughlin of all detail once he had taken his shots. He and the photo service already had agreements as to marketing, royalties, and fees, made long before. All he had to do was to turn over his negatives, leaving the distribution of prints to Wide World.

The next McLaughlin yarn is too good to omit, though its lesson is obscure, except that it proves the old adage "there is more than one way to skin a cat."

Long before World War II, one of the national magazines offered him an assignment to make air views at a Federal installation approximately 600 air miles from his home base at Curtiss Field. But their top offer for the job was only $300. That was barely enough to cover plane hire from New York and return, leaving no margin for lay-over time, profit, and expenses. Of course there might be subsequent sales to other publications but that seemed a bit too speculative.

The problem was how to do the job for $300 and still make an immediate profit. Here's how McLaughlin solved it.

Instead of flying Mac got into his old car and without stopping for sleep drove the more than 600 miles by road in twenty-four hours. Rather tired, he reached the city nearest the assignment spot early in the morning. There he hired a plane. The rate was $20 an hour. The whole photographic flight took exactly a half hour, so the plane cost was $10. His pictures made, Mac, still without sleep, got back into his car and started the grueling drive home to New York.

Meanwhile the magazine had been calling his office to ask when he would get in with the pictures. His staff, not too truthfully, made vague excuses about thick weather and bad photographic conditions at the assignment spot. They said that he had been delayed but would be back the next day, if the "weather" cleared up. McLaughlin got back the next day, but on the ground, not in the air. The pictures were delivered and a handsome profit realized, but it took Charley a week to rest up from the forty-eight-hour grind over the highways without sleep or rest.

Though there was some subterfuge, no one really suffered from the roundabout way of reaching the picture objective. McLaughlin worked out a feasible method of producing the pictures the magazine wanted within budget limitations. Flying from 10 miles away instead of 600 miles didn't affect the quality of the photographs. All it did was delay delivery of the finished pictures. That might have made the editors, nearing their deadline, a little jumpy, but certainly did no real hurt.

Another old-timer at aerial pictures is Robert A. Smith. As long as we can remember, Smith, generally known as Captain Bob (a World War I rank), has been operating a camera for Fairchild Aerial Surveys. And he is still at it. He also has many pertinent tips for the budding aerial photographer.

His first bit of advice is, unless you are striving for some particular and unusual effect, don't shoot directly into the sun from an airplane. Normally that advice applies equally well when both feet are planted firmly on the ground.

Next in importance, he thinks, is extreme accuracy in the location of shots made from the air. That is essential in mapping, but it is very important, too, when making obliques. The photographer should be so definite about location that he can describe the scene of his picture accurately in his caption and be able to pinpoint it on a map. As an example, Smith cites getting the caption information for an aerial shot of a traffic accident. If the mishaps occurred on a numbered highway, the road number should be given as well as the direction and distance to the nearest major intersection or city. Just suppose a cameraman flying over the Valley of Virginia spotted a smash-up on a road below. In his caption he should identify the location this way: "Fifteen miles south of Roanoke, Virginia, on Route 11."

Smith is very much in agreement with McLaughlin on the advisability of making aerial pictures as the plane approaches the objective. Physical features of earlier aircraft made it necessary to shoot toward the rear of the plane. That meant all the photographs had to be made going away from a scene. But present-day plane construction permits the approach technique.

Smith also agrees that it is sometimes necessary to depart from the rule against shooting into the sun. To do that successfully requires wider lens apertures than when the sun is behind the camera. Every photographer knows that, because it is equally true for ground shots, though aground the problem of getting more light on the film can also be solved by slower shutter speeds. When shooting with the sun from a plane, all surfaces of buildings and other objects in an oblique aerial are brilliantly lighted. But when the target is approached with the plane pointed directly into the sun, the sides of the buildings will be in deep shadow. The only practical way of getting sufficient exposure is to open the lens wider. The speed of the plane prevents using slower shutter speeds to get more light on the negative.

Working as he does with specially designed aerial cameras, Captain Bob recommends 1/300th or faster as ideal shutter speed. And that of course is for occasions when the weather is fine, with plenty of strong sunlight. Adverse weather naturally will call for adjustments of shutter speeds and lens openings, preferably the latter.

Like all cameramen, Smith has run into situations where pictures had to be made right away, with no opportunity to wait out the bad weather. Many times he has used shutter speeds as slow as 1/50th of a second. Smith has also made aerial shots at much slower speeds, but never on assignments, only on tests to learn techniques that might be helpful when pictures had to be made under very adverse conditions. He has made pictures from a plane at shutter speeds of 1/10th of a second. Only 10 percent of these were usable; too much motion spoiled the other 90 percent. That information should prove valuable for an assignment when news pictures must be made and waste of materials is less important than getting the pictures that won't wait for the weather. However, on normal assignments such a practice is not only too wasteful, it is also too speculative when excellent photography, rather than news value, is the prime requirement.

While on the subject of lens apertures and shutter speeds, Smith recommends that the tyro in aerial photography use an exposure meter. Until a photographer becomes as familiar with light intensities several thousand feet up as he is with sunlight on the ground, an exposure meter will save a lot of film.

Smith also recommends care in picking the pilot for an aerial assignment. He points out that finding a pilot who knows how to fly for pictures is almost a prime essential. For example, working at extremely slow shutter speeds requires not only a steady hand on the part of the photographer but highly skilled cooperation on the part of the pilot. He must keep the plane flying smoothly. Indeed, an experienced pilot can contribute much to the success of any aerial photographic assignment.

"Get acquainted with the local charter pilots," Smith advises. "Try to find out which of them have flown on photographic jobs. The pilot's knowledge about how to come in for a photographic run, how to keep the plane level, and other tricks of the trade have much to do with the success of any aerial picture job."

For the camera-carrying traveler riding on scheduled airliners for pleasure or business, Captain Bob also has some suggestions. He recommends that the camera be small, minicam size or at largest not bigger than a Rollei. Shooting through plane windows produces good pictures, if beforehand you make certain that the window is clean. The photographer should be on the watch for handprints and other smudges. They may not look like much, but they will show up disastrously on the negatives.

Smith himself has never run into spot news or feature pictures on such passenger trips but he is always alert. And unless the weather has closed in, such trips are never wasted photographically. He has made a collection of stock views and scenes, both in 16-millimeter movies and on still negatives. He recommends that the flying photographer, and especially the cameraman who pilots his own plane, carry along a small movie outfit. For if the pilot-photographer happens to fly over a fire or something else that might make a news picture, with a movie camera he would have a doubled sales opportunity. Stills, either made with a separate camera or blown up from the movie strip, might be marketed for publication, while the movie sequence could be offered to newsreels and television.

Though Smith was reluctant to discuss news exploits, he did mention one. And that provides a curious coincidence, because he claims a picture beat on the *Muenchen* fire. McLaughlin's account has been recorded. Now compare it with Smith's recollection of the same news story.

Strangely enough, these two keen rivals in aerial photography were flying mapping jobs the same day and almost at the same hour. Smith was finishing his task as McLaughlin was starting.

About the time McLaughlin's pilot was banking to straighten out over the West Side Highway, Smith's pilot was turning over Morristown, New Jersey, for the run back to the home field on Long Island. As the plane turned east, the two men saw a plume of smoke rising from New York Bay.

The pilot immediately nosed his craft down and flew toward the smoke. By the time they were over the harbor they were low enough for close-up shots of the burning ship. Smith made eight or ten obliques and then the plane streaked for Roosevelt Field. Immediately upon landing the roll of aerial film was rushed to the Fairchild laboratory in Long Island City for processing.

Meantime Smith had telephoned Times Wide World Photos in New York City. By the time the film had been developed and dried, and the fire shots separated from the mapping sequence, a motorcycle messenger was waiting, ready to rush the negatives to Times Square.

Both Smith and McLaughlin are certain that they beat everybody who got into the air after the fire report reached the news offices. That is undoubtedly true. But which of them reached Wide World first, I don't remember. I should, because it was part of my job to keep contact with both of them for aerial news breaks. As occasionally happened, they may have been so close that we used something from each of them. That happened on more than one story. But though they have put me right into the middle of this one, I don't know the answer.

Before we pass along some more advice from the specialists in aerial photography, let's pick up a few pointers from another newsman who, although his regular beat is on the ground, has made many air shots. He is Murray Becker, chief photographer of the Associated Press. Nowadays when Becker flies to make pictures like those of the fatal railroad wreck at Woodbridge, New Jersey, early in 1951, he uses a regular aerial camera. But in the early days he used a Graphic.

For most newsmen who go up in a plane for an occasional picture, the problem was then, as it still is, how to keep air pressure from depressing the bellows of the camera and throwing everything out of focus. Normally air views on news stories are made by leaning over the side of open-cockpit planes or out of a window of cabin jobs. In either case there is a great deal of air rushing by.

Standard aerial cameras have cones to protect the lens and focusing mechanism. Becker approximated that by folding a piece of tin or other light metal to form two sides and a top, just large enough to cover the bellows of his camera. It was open at the bottom and at both ends. At the front holes were bored in either side of the device; these fitted over the screws on the front standard of the camera. Tightening the screws fastened the shield securely. Though homemade, the tin shield did a satisfactory job of protecting the flexible bellows from air pressure.

We can take another leaf out of Becker's book, this one concerning his flight to photograph the Woodbridge wreck. The slower the cruising speed of the plane, the better off is the photographer. He can use slower shutter speed if the aircraft isn't rushing past the ground too fast. Therefore for the Woodbridge assignment a small, slow-speed plane was chartered. The wreck occurred after dark so the air views had to be made the following morning.

That day was windy—so blustery in fact that the small plane found a headwind was blowing at the same rate as the craft's top speed. For a while the plane hovered motionless in the air almost like a helicopter. Becker says they were standing still in the air though the propeller was going full speed. Then the wind got stronger and the plane, engine still at full throttle, began to slip back. So the pilot turned around and landed at his home airport.

Next a higher-speed cabin ship was chartered for the picture flight. It got to the wreck scene all right, but because weather and therefore light were bad, it had to come down very low for the air shots. And Becker had to hold his heavy aerial camera out of the window for the pictures. His arms were sore for days from the strain of holding the outfit clear of contact with the plane cabin to avoid transmitting motion that might produce movement on his negatives.

In Philadelphia veteran pilot and aerial photographer Virgil Kauffman heads the oldest company that operates with the use of aircraft. He is president and principal owner of Aero Service

Corporation, which started to carry passengers and freight in 1919. It switched to aerial photography early in the twenties. Right now making oblique photographs—the kind used in publications—is a sideline that costs more than it brings in. But it gives Kauffman an excuse to shuck executive duties, get away from his desk, and fly his own low-altitude picture assignments.

In spite of the load of company management, Kauffman has never wholly stopped being an aerial photographer, and has some pertinent advice to offer everyone faced with the problem of making news pictures from the air. Most opportunities, or at least the less costly ones, will come to cameramen traveling on scheduled airliners, so he starts with some pointers for those who wish to make shots through passenger-plane cabin windows.

"Unfortunately," says Kauffman, "most commercial airliners fly very high, where there is much haze. That means, first, that long focal-length cameras are needed because the objectives are so tiny. Second, the tremendous wing span of modern airliners blocks the perspective angle on both sides of the cabin. The best place for anyone trying for pictures on such flights is the number one place up front. Next best are the seats farther back. In those positions the wing is not directly below the window and therefore not directly in the line of view.

"If the airplane is very high and riding smooth, the photographer can work as slow as 1/100 of a second. Don't expect to do too much with color from commercial airliners unless a subject is brilliant, close, and a color-haze filter is used. The last is essential. Otherwise the transparencies will have a disagreeable bluish cast due to the invisible ultra-violet light which affects color film."

Though news assignments helped to keep his company in business in the early days, Kauffman got out of aerial news photography a long time ago. Making oblique views for industrial purposes paid better, and flying conditions were more satisfactory. Now even that is a sideline, handled only to help out old customers. Topographic mapping and airborne magnetometer surveys for underground and underwater deposits of minerals and oil are his company's major endeavors.

As a matter of personal observation, Kauffman feels the older a flyer gets, the less interested he is in covering news from the air. All too often the news breaks occur when the weather is most unfavorable for safe flying and getting good pictures. As to how to make news photos, Kauffman concurs in the main with Bob Smith of Fairchild. He particularly endorses Smith's advice about good size and knowing exact location. He also agrees that getting a pilot with experience in guiding a craft on a picture flight is important. It is exceedingly difficult, he knows, for even the most experienced cameraman to guide a pilot who has never flown a photographic flight.

Though making industrial pictures from the air is a highly specialized business (and he doesn't recommend that it be attempted hit or miss) Kauffman offers some points for those who wish to try it. And the advice applies equally well to making good news shots from an airplane.

"Industrial photography," says Kauffman, "should be of the highest quality for the uses to which it is put; therefore, it becomes imperative that the best of photographic equipment and techniques be used in getting pictures for top use. It is the experience of most people who make commercial photographs that properly made pictures can bring the highest prices. Pictures made with small cameras and poor flying produce poor photography and are worth little more than the paper they are printed on.

"Cameras used in commercial work are capable of taking pictures approximately 8 by 10 inches in size and are of extremely rugged construction for rough handling." (We'll interrupt here to say for these reasons Aero Service builds its own cameras. Some of them used in the surveys are constructed to rigid instrument specifications for that single purpose.)

Now, let's get back to Kauffman's advice: "For good pictorial obliques, shutter speeds should run from 1/300 to 1/400 of a second. Since most commercial pictures are made under favorable weather conditions and reasonably close to the subject, filters such as the K2 or minus blue are more than adequate. The heavier the filter, the greater the contrast will be, with resultant loss of details in the shadows. Infra-red, except for covering great areas from high altitude or in exaggerated cloud effects, is not practical.

"Perspective is of great importance. In industrial work the plant manager or president of the company wants to have workshops and surroundings appear in their most favorable light. It is essential, therefore, that the camera be placed in position for proper perspective showing the front and part of the sides of the lay-out. If the plane is flown too high, you get too much roof and not enough of the sides of the buildings; if you fly too low, you don't get any perspective of depth, and buildings in the background are oftentimes completely obscured. It is most important on assignments of this kind for the picture maker to know the preferred angle of the customer. Then the photographer has to evaluate this problem with the knowledge of sun angle, etc., and get over the location at about the right time. That is very important. Sometimes the exacting demands of the customer are such that it is a good thing for the photographer to circle around the job site to familiarize himself with the requirements and to plan his proper photographic approaches.

"The usual method of taking oblique photographs of this kind is with a slow aircraft flown by a capable pilot, with the photographer directing the operation. The best pictures are made with a minimum of vibration, and it is oftentimes of value to have both the power and speed of the plane reduced while the plane is flying a straight line to the camera point. This could be very dangerous with inexperienced flight people at low altitudes. And in the past quite a few overly ambitious photographers have come to a quick end in such practices.

"We in Philadelphia, with continuous problems in this sort of work, have cut the requirement of two men going in the aircraft by using a photographic pilot for the work. Usually I am that photographer-pilot. The camera is properly shock-mounted so that its angle of view just misses the propeller tip. The camera, which is electrically controlled, is remote from the pilot. Using coordinated sights in the cockpit, the pilot approaches the picture subject in a shallow glide. When the objective fills the view finder, he presses a release on the control column and a solenoid trips the camera shutter. In some camera installations, the pilot can reach around and wind the film for the next exposure; in others, the film-wind is automatic. Sometimes three or four shots can be made on one approach, cutting down time and risk at low altitudes.

"All the foregoing refers to oblique picture-taking only. Vertical photography is another phase of aerial work. Though seldom used in news or the kind of commercial aerial photography I have been discussing, it has become an art and science of great importance in map making," Kauffman goes on. "This vertical photography is the foundation of making maps to exacting specifications by 'photogrammetric' means. That's a new word. 'Photogrammetric' simply means accurate measurement by photography. It is in current dictionaries.

"Today practically all mapping of large areas is made by photogrammetric methods. The vertical aerial photography will probably not be more than 5 or 10 percent of the total job, but this aerial photography is like the foundation for a building—if it is improperly made, the resultant map is just as inaccurate as a building on a shaky foundation. This art and science is so developed that exacting maps are made by this process showing the various evaluations of the terrain as close as one foot vertically. In this case the cameras have to be built to the standards of engineering instruments. A recent quotation for new six-inch lenses for mapping cameras was $5,900 per lens, plus the 25 percent tax. Companies like ours in this line of work have great investments in equipment and trained personnel. To make these pictures properly, it is necessary that the operating aircraft be the most efficient ships for flights at high altitudes under extremely cold and thin air conditions, where oxygen must be supplied for hours at a time. The photographer's technique includes a knowledge of flying, since photographic techniques and methods require his determining the exact flight path. He must orient his camera in that path even though, owing to heavy cross-winds, the aircraft headings are many degrees to the left or right of the true flight path! His exposure must be exactly computed so that not only does he get the highlights, but also the shadows from the hillsides and buildings, which must be reproduced. Even more important, the pictures have to be made in a sequence so that a geometric pattern is produced for the engineer working on them in the stereo plotting equipment—a step in converting what is recorded on the photographic film to a finished map.

"Though I have gotten away from news obliques," Kauffman continues, "some of the incidents and close shaves that added a fillip to that activity are still memory fresh. I don't recall the exact year, but I do remember that *Life* magazine gave me a Fourth-of-July assignment to picture from the air the Ringling Brothers circus at New Bedford, Massachusetts. I flew up in the afternoon, and though it was rainy, we planned to take pictures about 2 P.M. But we hadn't counted on the circus roustabouts. They were on strike.

"However, we flew around until we ran out of gas. We were using a seaplane and landed in the bay. Aviation fuel wasn't available, so we bought some automobile gasoline and flew back over the circus. It wasn't fully dark, but the circus lights were on in the twilight of that dismal afternoon. With the lens wide open I shot at 1/10 of a second. And *Life* bought the picture!—for $150.

"Taking pictures from low-flying aircraft has its excitement because there are navigational hazards of flying aircraft across country. Air is always rough at low altitudes when the weather is clear, particularly so around smokestacks, buildings, and industrial areas.

"Years ago we had a picture to take in the Pennsylvania mountains. I had with me an old chum. We had taken the door off this fast little monoplane, and he sat to my right with the camera in his lap. We had pictures to take in those mountains for certain utilities, showing general terrain, etc. We were flying very low, with the camera pointed through the open doorway.

"It was a turbulent day, and this friend had done very little flying. All I wanted him to do was click the shutter when I signaled. The engine was running something like the way engines do in very old cars on dry days! He asked how I could tell the direction the wind was blowing. I told him to look at the trees and see how they were bending on the ridge below us.

"Then he said, 'You have been flying a long time. Did you ever have a bad forced landing?' Just then every instrument on the panel started dancing. There was a terrific explosion. Hot oil came back over both of us. Daylight disappeared as loose cowling flapped over the windows and black oil covered them. As I pushed out the window, the airplane went into a stall, but by pushing ahead on the stick, we were able to regain flying speed. My friend yelled, 'My God! Are the wings off?' I answered, 'No, but the engine is gone.' And it was. He then said to me, 'Now is the time to show me you can really fly.'

"There was no place to land but a little green spot on the edge of the river, and I got to it running as fast as I could go. I cut my hands trying to shut off the gas. We slipped between some rocks and the trees and flattened out on what turned out to be a small stretch of rye. The airplane made a normal landing on its belly because when the engine left, it sliced off the undercarriage. We stopped within a distance of 150 feet without further damage. That happened in the vicinity of Haycock Mountain, not too far from Bethlehem, Pennsylvania.

"Another time I was taking pictures, I picked a very nervous pilot. He was an old-timer. Our mission was to go up along the Susquehanna to photograph some islands in the river. We were flying one of those open-cockpit airplanes in which you get up and lean over to take the pictures. Then the pilot throttles the motor, you get back into position, change the plate, and get up to take another one. When we got a few miles south of Williamsport, Pennsylvania, there was the large island we were assigned to photograph.

"I went through the usual procedures, took the picture with the engine throttled, changed the plate, and then I noticed the pilot didn't answer when I said, 'Okay, Ben.' Nothing happened, and I noticed the mountains right there were sticking up way above us. I wanted to get moving, away from there, but my pilot was out of sight. Finally his head came up from the forward cockpit and he announced, 'The damn thing has quit on us.' The throttle control system had broken and he had been on the floor of the cockpit trying to fix it. He didn't succeed, so we made a forced landing in the smallest corn patch I ever saw. Once safely on the ground, we fixed the throttle and flew on.

"Our vertical mapping expeditions are not without dangers and incidents worth remembering. Joseph Mullen, our chief pilot, was in Mozambique on an exploratory mapping flight some time ago. It had nothing to do with the assigned job, but he wanted to get some air pictures of the wild elephant herds in Aramputo, about an hour's flight from our base of operations. Since he wished to get close, he borrowed a small plane from a Portuguese flying club. All went well until they got over those elephants at about 100 feet altitude. Then the engine started to sputter. Joe got a picture or two, but in no time at all the propeller and undercarriage were cutting the high reeds. And the elephants were charging directly at the plane. By good luck the engine picked up sufficient power to let them finally climb away and fly back to Lourenço Marques, the capital of Portuguese East Africa.

"The interesting thing in photographing elephants from a plane is that the bulls will break lose from the herd and charge at the aircraft. They throw their trunks high in the air, bellowing so loudly that I have heard them above the noise of the engine of the airplane."

So far, we have heard only from men who have taken photographs from the air. Now we come to some advice in the form of experience anecdotes from a pilot who has flown many picture flights for cameramen. He is J. Victor Dallin, chief of the Bureau of Aeronautics of Philadelphia, Pennsylvania. For many years he operated his own aerial service in Philadelphia, and we bought a great many pictures from him. Of course Dallin made his own pictures a good deal of the time. He probably was the first man to mount an aerial camera on the wing of a plane so that he could fly and take photos alone.

But we will let him speak for himself. "My experience in aerial photography," writes Dallin, "began first with the Royal Flying Corps during the first world war. It was not until July of 1919, when I was released from the service, that I took up commercial aerial photography, which more and more interested me as time went on, and finally, early in 1920, being perhaps the earliest pioneer in the U. S. A., I began almost exclusive aerial photographic operations which were carried on until the beginning of World War II.

"When you are making clothes, houses, and many other things

which may be offered to the general public for sale, almost anyone is interested in what you have to offer; but when you make an aerial photograph, very few are interested in its purchase unless it happens to be a picture of something of very general interest. Therefore, aerial photographs, taken on speculation, invariably cannot be profitably sold unless they are of a subject of general interest. Besides, when you make an aerial photograph on a speculative basis, the owner of the property invariably feels that you were merely skylarking with a camera and happened to snap his property. He is under no obligation to buy, and in many cases he will feel resentful at your intrusion and your suggestion that he consider your picture unless it was made on a contract basis.

"In aerial photography the pilot is most important, as position is everything. If he does not have an understanding of what the photographer is trying to do and cannot get at the proper height and position to the subject, and wherever possible use the wind to favor a reduction of ground speed, it is almost impossible for the photographer to accomplish much coordination in the air except by resorting to hand signals. These are always easy to arrange on the ground but difficult to accomplish during flight with noise of engine and lack of communication.

"Beginning in 1919, and for many years thereafter, I used a 90-horsepower JN4C aircraft for this work. It had two open cockpits, the pilot flying from the rear and the photographer operating from the front. It was extremely windy and became more so whenever the photographer got up into the slip stream, as he invariably did in the taking of pictures. Another general condition which you constantly find in aerial photography is that the best photographic weather usually follows heavy rains when the atmosphere is thoroughly washed, thereby providing the best visibility. However, usually following such a condition, one encounters high winds and severe bumpiness, often resulting in increased ground speed, particularly when the aircraft has to approach a subject in a downwind direction.

"I well recall a condition such as the above at Toronto, Ontario. The photographer at that time was Sidney Bonnick, who then was probably the most experienced aerial photographer in

America. Attempting flight in an extremely windy condition in the underpowered Canadian Jenny was always an ordeal, and only after considerable delay could one reach 1,000 feet altitude. On this particular occasion when we finally reached that height, the photographer turned around and informed me with evident embarrassment that he had left his camera on the ground.

"On another occasion, when photographing Niagara Falls and endeavoring to obtain the most intimate pictures of the Horseshoe Falls, Bonnick signaled for lower position and finally the aircraft got so low that the plane was almost sucked into the Niagara gorge. So I was involuntarily forced to proceed down the gorge under the bridges, making hairpin turns until a less turbulent air condition permitted the plane with its underpower engine to climb out. Bonnick, during the thrilling experience, kept shooting pictures over the aircraft tail and got some remarkably unusual views of the Falls and the bridges. Not until after the flight ended did he realize that the aircraft was actually unable to climb any higher; perhaps if he had, some of the resultant pictures would not have been so well made.

"In those early days, we used nothing but glass plates for our negatives, and I remember one day in particular when, after two hours of skylarking at low altitude in very high winds and bumpy air, the photographer en route to the studio admitted leaving the exposed plates in the airport streetcar. Eventually they were turned in to the streetcar company and no one had been curious enough to pull the black slides to see what was inside, or all our work would have been in vain.

"In pioneering in those days, as we went from town to town, we had to improvise photographic darkrooms which usually were made by use of the modern hotel bathroom. And since we were using at that time pyro-metol stain developer, it was always a horrible sight to look on the stained bathtub, which had to be thoroughly washed before the maid arrived on the scene lest we get thrown out for improper use of such facilities. Perhaps only those who have used pyro-metol developer can appreciate the resultant stain. Iodine immediately comes to my mind.

"One time we were photographing Atlanta, Georgia, and prior to taking the country estate of a millionaire there, it was suggested that Bonnick and I mount some of their valuable horses and ride over the place early in the morning with the engineer for familiarization purposes. Upon learning that Bonnick had never been on a horse, the engineer decided against that procedure, and when I protested, he replied, 'I am not worried about Bonnick staying on the horse as much as I am of having the horse run away!' In other words the horse in his opinion was far more important than the aerial photographer.

"One of the most embarrassing experiences I had in the reproductive use for magazine work was with the *National Geographic Magazine*. Owing to the plate having been put in with the glass toward the subject, the resultant photograph of the City of Los Angeles, unless deliberately reversed in the printing processes, naturally came out backward. This I knew but in spite of the warning written on the negative envelope, a print from that reversed negative was inadvertently reproduced in the *National Geographic Magazine*, and the complaints from the horror-struck Los Angeles people caused the editors to demand their money back and an apology for tampering with the official lay-out of the City of Los Angeles. I often wondered how many residents of Los Angeles had viewed the picture of their own city without noticing such a discrepancy.

"During the latter part of 1919," Dallin continues, "one of the oldest photographers in the United States, the late William N. Jennings of Philadelphia, decided he would like to take up aerial photography, having made the first aerial photographs of Philadelphia from a balloon in 1896 when the famous City Hall was under construction. Since he was then over sixty years of age, his wife seriously objected. Convinced of the necessity for drastic action, he invited his wife and the three children to take their first ride with me. As we naturally picked a nice calm day, we gave them a demonstration of simple flying, which of course was not to be compared with the type of work that Jennings and I later did. However, that so impressed Mrs. Jennings that she agreed to let him fly *only with me*—and I am sure that the confidence he himself later developed in me was greatly misplaced, because he went anywhere with no apparent fear. My conscience bothered me when I knew that in some of the extremely low positions we had to fly into, engine failure (which was quite normal in those days) would have certainly resulted in a loss of confidence.

"Bill Jennings had a camera of his own design and construction which he jealously guarded more than his own life. He always strapped the camera in the front cockpit, but never took such precautions for himself. One day we were over Bryn Mawr College and I signaled him for a right-hand photograph, then because of excessive drift by the wind, resignaled for a left-position view. In scrambling around the cockpit with his bulky camera, he inadvertently got his foot caught in the choke wire—a very crude contraption in those days—and the engine naturally coughed and cut out. So in desperation I violently banked the plane, intending to sideslip unheralded upon the front lawn of a Main Line country estate. The violence of the maneuver caused Jennings to lose his balance, and he fell down in the front seat, camera and all, thereby releasing the choke wire and permitting the engine to function normally again, so that we got home safely. It was with extreme difficulty after we got back to the field that I could convince him that the unkind maneuver was not deliberate on my part and most unkind, inconsiderate, etc.

"Many times in those early years we received orders to photograph churches and hospitals and other institutions for promotional purposes where enlargement programs were under consideration. Invariably such institutions were located in built-up areas where photographing at low altitude was done with considerable trepidation. Syd Bonnick inadvertently double-exposed Methodist churches with such recurring regularity that he developed a phobia against photographing that type of subject, as it obviously meant going back and doing the work all over again.

"During our first winter in Atlanta, Georgia, the New York *Times*' Midweek Pictorial commissioned us to photograph Stone Mountain and also the KKK Palace in Atlanta. We had no difficulty in finding Stone Mountain, it being a national landmark; but every time we went around the north side with a prevailing south wind to try to photograph that part of the mountain where the proposed statues were to be carved, we received a most violent bump, spoiling the picture and throwing Bonnick against the upper wing. We had to make several wide circles of the subject before we got satisfactory photographs.

"In the case of the KKK Palace, all we received was a very exaggerated story about the elegant palace, the location of which had been placed upon an Atlanta city map. In our photo-aircraft, at a very low and dangerous altitude we went up and down Peachtree Street looking for it, and finally in desperation I instructed Bonnick to photograph a large house, the only place I could imagine that would correspond with the location. Fortunately it later proved to be the Palace, but it certainly was nothing like the newspaper stories concerning its grandeur and size.

"I endeavored to interest the New York Shipbuilding Corporation, Camden, New Jersey, in a photograph of the launching of the *U.S.S. Saratoga,* which was the first aircraft carrier, I believe. They decided that they would prefer to get the picture from the Navy, which was scheduled to cover the launching with great activities. Somehow I felt that they might not succeed in getting the picture. So, going against my belief that speculative work does not pay, I circled the New York Shipbuilding Yards along the Delaware River in spite of the fact that naval aircraft in formation were going up and down the river in great numbers. After what seemed an interminable delay, I looked down at the shipyard and suddenly saw the vessel descending the shipways into the Delaware, and the time being critical, I vertically banked our Jenny and sideslipped to get the photographer in position quickly. He succeeded in snapping two or three pictures before the ship got out into the river stream, where everyone had similar ideas and uncoordinated competition resulted.

"Little did I know at the time when I sold the picture to the New York *Times* and the Philadelphia Sunday *Public Ledger*, that the Navy would officially object to their publication. I shortly thereafter sold the picture to the New York Shipbuilding Corporation, which had failed to get something suitable from the United States Navy. Shortly thereafter I received a visit from a naval official protesting the publication of the picture and demanding to know to whom it had been sold. Unfortunately the New York Shipbuilding Corporation was forbidden by the Navy to make use of the picture and prior to this order they had bought the pictures, negatives and all. Previous to releasing the negatives, with their agreement I had struck from each one hundred contact prints for secondary sale through the Naval Stores. This plan was also nipped in the bud by official objection. Apart from the merchandising difficulties which ensued, it was one of the most hair-raising events in my career, in that naval aircraft from all directions were milling around us. How a collision was avoided, I do not know because we certainly had no business being where we were under the circumstances.

"On another occasion, after we photographed a summer hotel up along the St. Lawrence River, the manager upon examining the pictures discovered certain tracks in the rear of the hotel in the dense woods which he claimed were not there. Upon checking them, he found out that it was a path used by thieves who had methodically removed the hotel silverware down the bank to a rendezvous on the river, which otherwise might never have been discovered. 'Photographs tell the story.'"

Captions Sell Pictures

GET THAT PICTURE IS TOO often the only thought of the cameraman covering a story. That's important all right, but it isn't all-important. There is much more to covering a picture story than getting the action in focus, setting lens stops and exposure time, and snapping the shutter.

The photographer who wants to sell his pictures to newspapers and magazines must always remember that covering an assignment is a two-part operation. The first part—and we don't want to underestimate its importance—is indeed getting the picture. But the second and equally important part is securing facts for captions or cut-lines. News cameramen, professionals as well as amateurs, are prone to forget at times that they are not just photographers. They are photographer-reporters and as such should put as much emphasis upon getting the story in words as they do upon getting the pictorial part of it on film. Of course you must go after the picture first, but don't consider your job is done when you've made a good exposure.

In over twenty years in various photo editorial capacities, I have turned down or have seen others turn down excellent shots simply because the words that would complete the story were missing. That hurt the contributing photographers, and it hurt us. No one likes to pass up a swell photograph, but what can you do when the information that would make it understandable is not available? And don't charge that off to editorial laziness. I and others in similar spots have spent hours consulting reference books, morgue clippings, and old wire reports in fruitless efforts to garner enough caption information to carry submitted photographs.

At the risk of seeming repetitious, I want to emphasize that in a very real sense everyone who wishes to succeed in making news pictures must be a reporter. For whether you do it as an avocation, part-time or full-time occupation, covering picture-news assignments is real reporting. The man with the camera has the additional chore of supplementing his picture with just as many facts as those other reporters who confine their activities to getting the story in words alone. So, until someone invents a tape recorder that will put a sound track on still negatives, the news cameraman must carry pencil and paper as well as his photographic gear.

Pictures often are very dramatic and almost self-explanatory, but never entirely so. Sometimes they need only a very few words to help. But can you remember any publication ever using pictures without some caption? You are going to ask: "Why, if a very striking photograph will carry just a brief caption when used in newspapers and periodicals, must I submit complete information when I make a knockout shot? Why wouldn't a short, snappy headline be much better?"

The answer requires explanation of some of the processes a picture passes through on its journey from you to the printed page. If you were not only photographer-reporter but editor as well, you could stop with the brief wording suited to your particular publication needs. But in reality you are only the man on the scene trying to record the story on a piece of film. Whether you submit it directly to a publication or through a picture agency, many editorial eyes will scan and consider your offering. Upon each editor that picture will make a different impact. Some editors may react as you do; other reactions may differ radically. Words will help get your own reaction across to all these people. Remember, too, that each publication has its own fairly rigid editorial rules as to picture treatment, including size of cut-lines, and sometimes those sizes require a lot of words to fill them.

So the man who wants to sell his pictures for publication must compromise. If he can compose a snappy catchline he should by all means do so. But he shouldn't stop there; he should also get all the facts and write them down. Within limits, which are usually governed by the size of the sheet of paper it is practical to attach to photographs about seven by nine inches, at least basic information is always supplied with their photos by the major picture services like AP News Photo, Acme Newspictures, and International News Photos.

There is an old journalistic rule taught to cub reporters that cameramen should learn too. Get the answers to these five questions and you have the heart of the story: "Who, What, Where, When, and Why?" Make certain that your picture captions include the answers to all five and you're off to a good start.

You will be building upon sand if you assume that because your local paper has printed a full story of an occurrence or because the wire services have sent out a report, the editor who receives your photographs will have all the details at his finger tips. It's a hundred-to-one shot that he won't. News is a most transitory commodity; yesterday's news is very dead tomorrow —and necessarily forgotten by a busy editor dealing with hundreds of fresh news breaks each day. Yet it will ordinarily be tomorrow before he receives your photos, for normally pictures, unless they are enormously important, lag behind the news moving on press-association wires. This is because no matter how small your town may be, a story can be telephoned or telegraphed to the remote corners of the world in a matter of minutes.

Pictures also move by wire, but the wire points are relatively few; it may be some time before you can get your pictures to the transmitter, and transmission may take additional time. So the lag between the arrival of the story and the arrival of the first picture can be very great. In that interval the wire copy detailing the news story may well have vanished in the paper jumble of the typical disordered city room. There is also the possibility that a story important in Oscaloosa may have no national news interest and therefore not have been moved on press-association wires; yet your pictures may be so dramatic that, important or not, they will be bought—if you have provided the editor with enough facts to explain them to people who have not heard of the event.

How long a caption should be will depend to a great degree upon the subject and the photographs. Obviously, if you are submitting a striking shot of a forked bolt of lightning, notation of the place and time it occurred and, if there was damage, the name of the place or persons hit should be sufficient. However, if there were freak results, by all means mention them, because that kind of information will add to the newsworthiness of your photographs. Don't overload your captions with descriptive adjectives, but don't hesitate to include every bit of fact you can supply. Don't depend upon the editor to fill in news about your picture from other sources. Names, correctly spelled (which photographers seem to be especially sloppy about), are very important, and so are addresses. Don't be satisfied with generalities such as state or cities; get street addresses whenever possible. Generally, it is best to list the names of those pictured from left to right. There are times when a group is too mixed up for that system to be best. Then use any method that will be understandable to the person receiving your pictures and captions. But no matter what method you use, clearly indicate in your caption whether people are identified from left to right, front to back, or some other way. No editor wants to guess at identifications and none of them will feel safe in assuming that you are using the conventional left-to-right method unless you say so.

Often information is omitted from captions because the cameraman thinks it is self-evident to anyone looking at the pictures. That, too, can be a very serious mistake. Seldom do any two persons see the same thing in a picture. If there is something in your picture that you think makes it outstanding or is important to the incident depicted, say so. You may lose the sale if you don't. No editor will resent attention-calling like that. He may and probably will see things in your photograph that you do not. That's all to the good. But don't take any chances on his failing to catch anything you think will help sell the picture for you.

Never lose sight of the fact that you're trying to sell that picture. So make it easy for editors to buy your pictures. Tell them not only what the picture shows, but as much of the background of the event as you can. There is little profit in going to bat with two strikes already called upon you. And that's just what you will be doing if you submit pictures with inadequate captions.

If you think this is an exaggeration, read these paragraphs

from a recent letter (October 31, 1950) written by Eleanor Ohsol, who edits the Acme Roto Service.

"I'm enclosing one set of captions and story that I did recently. . . . This horrible example, of course, may be a bit unfair because the story came all the way from New Zealand, but I think it illustrates the point that you should not take for granted what your editors (or your readers) might or might not know.

"I had to do a terrific amount of research to get the story, since all I had to go on were the brief captions on the clipping and the briefer individual captions on the backs of the prints. Naturally the clipping was from a New Zealand paper, and presumably the readers in New Zealand are familiar with the folklore and history of the Maori, but the rest of us ain't.

"It might be well for the out-of-town photog to take note that some information as familiar to him as Maori folklore is to the average New Zealander would be as unknown to a New York editor as the Maori folklore is to the average American. It doesn't hurt to include the obvious sometimes, even if it's a corny title, a lead idea, or background information. The editor can easily delete or alter, but it's tough to add something to almost nothing."

Though Miss Ohsol's pithy comment covers the subject rather completely, I might add that the clipping from the New Zealand paper was simply the local reproduction of three pictures with cut-lines. I am willing to bet that the paper carried a story alongside the pictures, but Acme's contributor carefully cut it away.

I wish to remark, too, that Miss Ohsol's action in this case was exceptional. After office hours she spent a great deal of time checking encyclopedias and other reference works to get enough factual background to carry the Maori picture story. But don't count upon being as lucky as this New Zealand contributor. Most editors, including me, would have said "the hell with it." There just isn't time enough to do a lot of research under the pressure of producing a picture service. So play safe. Take nothing for granted. Include all the material you can. Catchy lines will help, but facts are the meat and potatoes of a good caption. Any editor can provide the trimmings, but the contributor must supply the main dish.

Now that it has been proved that complete captions are very

important and necessary if you wish to sell your pictures, let's consider the practical aspects of writing captions. The information you send along with spot-news shots will vary a bit from that required for features, but in the main the same rules apply to captions for both types of news pictures.

As spot-news pictures normally depict spontaneous happenings like fires, accidents, crimes, etcetera, we shall write a specimen caption about one of those—a fire. But before we start to write, in fact while we're still making the picture, we should consider what information is needed. First our caption should locate the scene: downtown, uptown, residential or business district, with the names of streets if on a corner, or the number and nearest cross-street if away from the corner. We should have a count of fatalities and injuries, extent of the damage, and, if available, some comparative data such as this being the largest fire since the so-many-thousand-dollar blaze so-many years ago. We should also tell how it started and what our picture shows, such as bodies dropping from windows, firemen swarming up ladders, a wall crumbling, or hoses playing on the flames.

With that information in hand we can write our caption. Typing is preferred, but in a rush pencil will do. And before we go any further I want to repeat: if you don't use a typewriter, *print all names.* Don't take a chance that your hurried scrawl can be read. Editors can often decipher badly scribbled words from the context, but that won't work with names. So print them and take no chances that might result in costly lawsuits if the name gets into type as *Perry* when you thought you were writing *Berry.* And always date your caption.

Here's the specimen caption for that imaginary fire.

> TEN LOST IN HOTEL BLAZE. Ten persons died this morning when the —— Hotel, in the heart of the downtown district of ——, Illinois, was gutted by fire. At least twenty others are in hospitals with burns and other injuries. According to fire chief James Jones, the blaze started in a utility closet on the main floor. It evidently smoldered for a long time before bursting into flame and mushrooming up through stair wells and elevator shafts. Chief Jones, immediately upon arriving at the scene, sent in the four-alarm signal, calling for all available apparatus. The

— Hotel at Sixth and Market Streets, built in 1925 at a cost of $500,000, is a total loss. Walls have bulged and the steel framework is twisted from the intense heat. No estimate has been made of the value of the furnishings, equipment, and personal property destroyed. This fire is the first fatal hotel blaze in this city since the Hotel — burned to the ground ten years ago with two fatalities.

This photo shows fireman John Smith carrying one of the injured down a ladder from an upper floor. 5/21/49

This is rather complete. You may not have time to get as many facts, especially if the only information sources available are the police and fire officials on the scene. But get as much as you can and be sure your caption contains all the information you do get.

You can and should do a much better caption job on feature pictures. Then you will not be under such intense pressure. There will be time to think and to check sources of information, some of which may not be correct or available at the scene. Quality in the photographs and the story told, both in words and pictures, are the prime requisites for features. The picture services have found that this means writing fairly long captions whether the feature consists of a single photograph or a series of shots. The basic idea is to provide enough text to run a short Sunday-magazine story or at least enough to use as a good-sized box in a picture-page lay-out. With that in view, the picture services devote more time to research and writing for features than for spot-news picture captions. The lead or main caption is really a short news-feature story. Depending upon subject matter, such captions will run as much as a thousand words. When I was on Wide World Photos we attached this long main caption to the best picture in the series. Acme, however, puts the main caption on a separate sheet, pasting only the individual captions to the prints. INP and Metro have individual styles in presentation, but the content is basically the same. Sometimes complete captions with cut-lines included at the bottom are attached to every photograph in the set.

The following captions, from a full-page picture spread in the New York *World-Telegram and Sun* during the spring of 1951, are typical of a feature lay-out:

SHAD ROW

MAIN CAPTION

The shad are running and in the shadows of George Washington Bridge fishermen are netting them for the market as they have for almost three hundred years. Each April the silver fish swim upstream to spawn, and every spring the Hudson River fishermen set their nets from the Jersey shore to points nearly halfway across the river. These pictures depict how the delicacy reaches your table.

PICTURE 1

The pointed poles on which the nets are strung are stuck into the river bottom about twenty feet apart. One can see them plainly from the West Side Drive.

PICTURE 2

The 500-foot nets present a real barrier to the shad. Shipping sometimes knocks down the poles and carries them away.

PICTURE 3

River traffic raises hob with nets. Here they are gone over for repairs at Floyd Clayton's on River Road, Edgewater.

PICTURE 4

Good eating coming aboard! Practically everyone has heard of shad roe.

PICTURE 5

Frank Nelson of Point Pleasant unloading a day's haul. Nets are set at low tide, hauled in on the high tide. Season's catch in normal years totals about 4,000,000 pounds.

PICTURE 6

Some of the catch is smoked on the scene—14 hours over hickory logs for that added flavor.

PICTURE 7

Mr. Clayton pours 125 pounds of buck shad into ice-packed wooden box for shipment.

PICTURE 8

And this is how the shad winds up, garnished with lemon and doused with piquant sauce.

These are the edited, finished captions as they appeared in the newspaper. Notice how all the leading persons in the pictures have been identified, not only by name but also by the towns in which they live. Note, too, the number of figures in the captions—the size of the nets, the distance between the poles, the total catch, and so on. These are the sort of facts that editors want, and it is a good bet that they were pleased if the photographer's original captions were at least twice as long and even more fact-filled.

Don't try to copy these for literary style or treatment; be yourself when you write. But do follow their lead upon the amount of information that is desirable. Tell your story simply, but tell it all. And don't forget to emphasize the parts you consider most important. As Miss Ohsol pointed out, if the contributor doesn't provide the information, the editor won't have much to go on.

It is not necessary to follow picture-service practice about pasting captions to prints. Instead you can put all the caption material on a separate sheet or sheets. Do whatever is handiest. But if you don't paste the captions and prints together, be sure that prints and captions have corresponding numbers so there is no doubt about which belong where.

If you still have any doubts about the dollars-and-cents results from doing as good a job on captions as you do on your photographs, I would like you to listen to Victor W. Talley, picture editor of the New York *Times* Sunday Magazine Section. He says:

"Very often the Sunday Magazine pays a contributor almost as much for the accompanying words as we do for the pictures. It is not too unusual for us to pay, where a cameraman has submitted a thousand words of good background material, $150 for five pictures and anywhere from $50 to $100 for the text.

"I can cite two excellent examples of that, both from the same contributor, Horace Bristol, who is covering the Korean fighting. The first appeared in the magazine on July 16, 1950. In twelve pictures which didn't need any text except what Bristol supplied for ample cut-lines, we told the complete story of the airlift from Japan to Korea. We gave it four full pages.

"The second occasion points up the importance of captions more dramatically. As usual, free-lance Bristol supplied ample background material with his set of photographs. The result was that we discarded all but two pictures, which were used as illustrations, but printed his caption data as a feature story from the front. With the illustrations, it rated a full page in the magazine of August 6, 1950. Bristol was paid top rates for an article."

Before we close this chapter on captions we want to emphasize an important item to be included in every caption. That is the date. You will have noticed that picture-service captions are always dated. The numerals at the end show the date the caption was written. If the caption describes spot news, words like "today," "yesterday," and "this afternoon" in the body of the caption will fix the time exactly. In feature captions the time lag between the taking of the picture and its publication use is greater, hence including the exact or almost exact time of the event or scene is often more important. So, in the body of the caption, tell just when the pictures were taken—last month, earlier in the year, last year, or last week. The more exact you can be, the better satisfied the receiving editor will be. There are times when old pictures make suitable subjects for current lay-outs. But identify them as old, with exact age if you can. Don't try to fool editors by pretending old pictures are recent productions. That's not only dishonest, but bad merchandising. You might make one sale, but you will be found out. And from then on everything you submit will be regarded with suspicion.

To sum up, captions are important—almost, but not quite, as important as the pictures they accompany. Without them it is virtually impossible to sell news pictures, either spot or feature. With good ones, your pictures will sell more readily. Captions should be concise but complete. If you will remember that you are telling a story when you make news pictures, that it is a two-part production, and that neither prints or words should be slighted, you will get best results. If your captions are good, your pictures will be better. And you will sell more photographs and get higher prices for them.

Selling to the Picture Services

AT THE START OF THIS book, the three major associations were listed as the best outlets for any cameraman lucky enough to be around when big news was breaking. Besides the big three, there are a couple of fair-sized outfits, Metropolitan and Wide World, in the feature field. Also there are a great many smaller agencies, which for the most part act as sales representatives for photographers, rather than as full-fledged picture services.

Now we shall proceed to study these and other picture services in greater detail. Knowledge of what they seek and how they want pictures submitted, plus a close look at some of their operations, should be helpful to the photographer who wants to sell news pictures.

Probably the best and widest market for spot-news photographs is the Associated Press. Its coverage is unrestricted by territorial limits. It gathers and distributes photographs all over the world. But the amateur and the semi-professional or professional free-lance who wants to sell pictures to AP must work fast. For AP primarily wants pictures that can move over its Wirephoto network in the United States simultaneously with or very soon after the written report of an event speeds on its teletypes. And AP's own sources of picture coverage are extensive.

Both in the United States and abroad, AP News Photos maintains full-time staff photographers at key bureau points. Besides that, it has ready access to the pictures made by the staff photographers of member newspapers. Yet many amateurs, lucky enough to be nearby when big news broke, have sold their pictures to AP and have been liberally rewarded. Among them has been Arnold Hardy, who made the remarkable pictures of falling bodies at the Winecoff Hotel fire in Atlanta. Another was a youngster who came into AP's New York office with pictures of a man knocked down by a taxicab; the victim proved to be the noted violinist Fritz Kreisler. And there have been a number of others.

If you want to be prepared to market spot-news pictures to AP, you should study the map of its Wirephoto network printed in this book. That will show you the shortest distance in miles or time (and time is more important) to one of its transmitting stations. If you get something good, communicate with that point if it is not too far away. If your local newspaper is a member of AP, it, very likely, will be glad to cooperate in making such queries. Sometimes that is an advantage, because while you may be a stranger to the men in the AP bureau, the newspaper editors are not. That often helps.

Because time, picture size, and picture quality are of prime importance in Wirephoto transmission, AP prefers to get negatives. Negatives save time for they eliminate copying to make reprints for Wirephoto and other distribution. And on hot stories don't wait to develop film; send it or bring it in undeveloped. While normally a 7 by 9 print will fit the Wirephoto drum, AP picture editors would rather make their own decisions on cropping and print size. Obviously you would be foolish to try to outguess them. And the faster your picture gets on the network and the better it looks, the more you will get for it.

The Wirephoto market for feature pictures is practically nonexistent. Wide World Photos, an AP affiliate, specializes in that phase of photography. We shall discuss its requirements later in this chapter. However, we might point out here that the best way for a free-lance photographer, whether amateur or professional, to submit pictures to Wide World is through the AP bureau nearest to him.

Next largest among the picture agencies is Acme Newspictures, with INP running a close third. But size alone is not always the best guide in picking potential customers for spot-news pictures. If your photos are absolutely exclusive, then you are in a position to choose any one of the three. Or if you shoot enough negatives and they are varied enough, you might be able to sell something to all three. On the other hand, and this is much more likely, you may find other photographers on the scene. In such a case try to learn whom they represent. If their pictures are going either directly or indirectly to one or two of the picture services, then your best chances would lie with whichever one has no one on the scene. There is good reason for this: the agency or agencies already protected are unlikely to be interested in seeing your pictures for possible purchase, while those that aren't covered are quite probably searching high and low for pictures on the story. Their editors will be very happy to get your query or to see you coming into the nearest office with your films.

Acme Newspictures has much the same set-up and requirements on spot news as AP News Photos. Acme is a division of NEA (Newspaper Enterprise Association) and it works closely with the United Press and the Scripps-Howard newspapers. It, too, has newspaper connections that permit picking up pictures which warrant wire transmission (Acme calls its system Telephoto) and it has its own full-time staff photographers spotted at strategic points and bureaus in the larger cities. The map of the Acme Telephoto leased-wire network is your guide to where to deliver spot-news shots for sale to Acme. Some of the Acme transmitting points, you will note, are in the same cities as the transmitters of the opposition. That is to be expected in big centers like New York, Washington, Philadelphia, Chicago, San Francisco, and Los Angeles. Their location, when they vary, is something else to keep in mind when you must decide quickly where to send a spot-news picture. The press association with the nearest transmitter might, for that reason alone, be your best market.

Unlike AP, Acme is a fairly good market for feature pictures as well as news shots. It uses single feature pictures in its daily mail service and sets in its Roto Service. Syndicate prices for feature pictures do not compare with those paid by the leading magazines and some of the top newspaper rotogravure sections. But that is often overbalanced by the quantity bought.

The Acme Roto Service production budget calls for distributing five feature sets weekly. These run from six to ten pictures on the average. Sometimes sets of less than six will be purchased and also on very rare occasions the top limit of ten will be exceeded. At least one, and occasionally two, of these weekly sets will come from free-lances. Eleanor Ohsol, editor of the Acme Roto Service, estimates that she buys about 75 such feature sets from contributors in the United States and abroad in the course of a year. Submitting negatives will help sell your set to her. They will be returned. Only rarely, and then with great reluctance, will Acme issue a feature series printed from copy negatives.

By and large, International News Photos, which is part of International News Service and very closely affiliated with the Hearst newspapers, has requirements, especially on spot news, that parallel those of its two principal competitors. As there are Hearst newspapers in most of the bigger cities, INP can get the pictures they produce as well as those made by its own staff photographers. Naturally that cuts down to some extent the amount of material purchased from outside sources. But to counteract that, each of the Hearst newspapers in its own territory is a prime market for spot-news pictures. The best of these pictures are likely to be picked up by INP, a fact which very often results in extra compensation for the contributing photographer.

INP's feature production is handled under the title By-Line Features. This title was chosen because it is practice to carry the name of the photographer, whether staffman or outsider, as the by-line at the top of the feature captions. Four By-Line sets are issued weekly. They run from six to twelve prints to the set. Most of them are conceived by INP editors and shot by INP staff photographers. Over the course of a year the purchases from outside sources will run rather low.

Now we come to the purely feature services. The older of them, Wide World Photos, operates as a division of the Associated Press, though it is organized as a separate corporation. With some exceptions, such as making photos to illustrate AP Newsfeature stories, Wide World is wholly in the feature end of picture production. It turns out a daily report that is mailed to a special list of subscribing members of the Associated Press. Included in its daily output are sets usually ranging up to four or five pictures but on rare occasions going as high as seven, plus a few single pictures of a semi-news feature nature. Besides features, fashions form a very important part of Wide World's output. In fact it is the only picture syndicate that emphasizes fashion coverage with a thorough job of issuing a fashion print service week in and week out. Acme includes fashions in its weekly budget too, but not so extensively.

The Wide World name is used for one other purpose. Those AP pictures which are sold for magazine and other publishing uses are marketed under the Wide World credit line by the commercial department of Wide World. But that doesn't widen the market for contributors. This explanation is made so those of you who note Wide World credits on spot-news pictures will not be misled into believing that it buys spot-news offerings.

Most of the WWP material is produced by AP staff photographers in the United States and overseas. A number of them are assigned full time to making pictures for Wide World. The quantity of pictures bought from contributors is very small, simply because the staff production is so high. Most of the outside pictures that are purchased are submitted through AP bureaus which forward them for final decision to Wide World headquarters in New York. In all cases no photograph will be purchased unless the original negative is available on loan. And in addition to other caption data, WWP insists on knowing the exact date upon which each photograph was made.

The other wholly feature picture service, the Metropolitan Group Editorial Service, at 220 East 42nd Street, New York 17, N. Y., deserves top place in any listing of markets for such photographs. You may have seen its pictures in rotogravure sections. They usually carry the credit line "Metro." At least half the shots it distributes are bought from contributing photographers. There is a simple reason for that. Metro doesn't have a single staff cameraman. The other half of its budget of photographs comes from Reuters, the British agency, for whose pictures Metro has North American newspaper rights.

Perhaps before we tell you what Metro wants, it would be well to tell you what Metro is. A little more than three years old, it is the latest entry into the picture service field. It was formed by a group of rotogravure editors to provide the type of single picture and picture-story sets needed for their Sunday editions. The roto editors of the papers it serves form the policy-directing board of

Metro. When this book was being put together, the Metro report was being mailed to thirteen Sunday rotogravure magazine sections with a total circulation of nearly 11,000,000. Nine of the subscribing papers were stockholder-owners of Metro's parent group.

We think you should know the names of these papers. It will be a partial guide to their position as possible markets for free-lances. For it is fairly obvious that roto editors receiving the Metro report will, to a greater or lesser extent, partly dependent on the size of their sections, restrict their purchases from contributors. This is the Metro list:

Boston *Globe,* 242 Washington St., Boston 7, Mass.
Buffalo *Courier-Express,* 787 Main St., Buffalo 3, N. Y.
Chicago *Tribune,* Tribune Sq., Chicago 11, Ill.
Cincinnati *Enquirer,* Cincinnati 1, Ohio
Cleveland *Plain Dealer,* 523 Superior Ave., N.E., Cleveland 14, Ohio
Detroit *News,* Lafayette Blvd. and 2nd Ave., Detroit 31, Mich.
Milwaukee *Journal,* 333 W. State St., Milwaukee 1, Wisc.
New York *Daily News,* 220 E. 42nd St., New York 17, N. Y.
Philadelphia *Inquirer,* Inquirer Bldg., Philadelphia 1, Pa.
Pittsburgh *Press,* Blvd. of the Allies, Pittsburgh 30, Pa.
St. Louis *Globe-Democrat,* 1133 Franklin Ave., St. Louis 1, Mo.
Toronto *Star,* 80 King St. W., Toronto 1, Ontario, Canada
Washington *Star,* 11th St. and Penna. Ave., N. W., Washington 4, D. C.

Some of these newspaper rotos, with the New York *News* a prime example, are still good markets for the independent contributor. Though the *News* gets the complete picture reports of the Associated Press, Acme, Wide World Photos, and Metro, and sees the output of every independent agency in New York, it also buys a good many black and white and color pictures from free-lance sources. Others, the Buffalo *Courier-Express* is one, buy very little in the way of feature lay-outs from outside contributors. If you are unsure about a Sunday newspaper as a possible market for your pictures, buy a copy. Turn to the picture sections and study the photographs. And watch the credit lines. They will indicate whether the pictures are all coming from established agencies or whether the independent is getting a break. And if that isn't conclusive, write a note and ask. The answer will tell you whether or not the editor wishes to see your pictures.

Unlike the big three in the picture service field, Metro does not touch spot news at all. Also, unlike them, it does not have a commercial department to sell its photos to such non-subscribers as weekly newspapers, magazines, house organs, advertising agencies, and others.

As a result, Metro does not want and does not buy full publication rights to photographs. All it asks are first North American serial rights and the same rights for the United Kingdom, where Reuters distributes its pictures. The contributor retains all resale rights. Often pictures have permanent value, and freedom to resell them can prove profitable to the photographer.

Correspondents may submit for consideration either prints or negatives to Metro. However, on acceptance, whether of a single photograph or a series, you must forward the original negatives. These will only be a loan, but Metro draws the line on making copy prints. In every case completely informative caption data are another important requisite. Literary style is not important. Metro editors will rewrite captions to suit their needs, but if you can put your best foot forward in the written presentation of your story, don't hold back. It will help your sales, not only to Metro but wherever else you submit photographs. The Metro editors don't mind getting queries about feature ideas before you make the pictures. They will tell you whether they think the project has possibilities for them. And if you have sold them pictures before, a query may bring back a definite assignment.

Though not a high-pay market, Metro makes up for that by buying a great many pictures during the course of a year. Its annual budget calls for the production of from four hundred to five hundred sets. This means that they purchase anywhere from two hundred to two hundred and fifty feature picture stories from independent contributors. That's a mighty big target to aim at. Also, and this is very important to the free-lance already employed in photography but anxious to spread out into the feature field, many cameramen who started out as contributors now get assignments from or through Metro.

In addition to the longer feature sets, which normally run from a half-dozen to a dozen pictures, Metro distributes about twenty individual feature photographs each week. The purchase ratio is the same as for series; about half are bought from amateurs or other free-lance contributors. And if you want to know more about the type of material Metro seeks, read the chapter on feature photography. If you can produce original picture stories along the lines indicated there, Metro should be an exceedingly good market outlet for you.

Because it is one of the few, if not the only, borderline agencies, we will next discuss European Picture Service, 353 Fifth Avenue, New York 16, N. Y. By borderline, we mean that European is to some extent a daily picture service like its much bigger brothers; its main business is acting as sales agent for independent photographers in the United States and abroad. Occasionally, some of the big three sell pictures on royalty arrangements, but this is a minor matter for them when they do it at all. On the other side of the scale, most of the independent picture agencies are primarily sales representatives. European deals in both service and sales.

Although they are loosely called syndicates and for our readers' convenience they are discussed here, most of the independent agencies are not press associations or syndicates at all. They are businessmen or companies filling the same role for the photographer that the author's agent does for the writer. They are middlemen trying to perform a sales service for the cameraman who does not have the time, the inclination, or the knowledge of picture markets to do it for himself. They charge a good fee for that service, usually 50 percent of the sales price. To a considerable extent, they are in constant touch with the potential market for a photographer's product. They often get much faster acceptances or rejections, through personal calls by salesmen, than can be obtained by the photographer through mail dealings. As part of their business they maintain picture libraries upon which editors call when they need pictures from file. If you produce scenic shots, city views, portraits, documentary photos, and other pictures of permanent value, sales from such files can prove profitable.

Cameramen, both amateur and professional, are not agreed upon the advantages or disadvantages of marketing through sales agents. We don't want to get into the middle of that argument. Our purpose is to present all the information, so each photographer can make the decision best suited to his own situation. For that reason, we will let Max Peter Haas, who owns and operates European, present the case for the agents who handle news feature pictures on a royalty basis. Though there may be some slight differences about minor details, in the main Haas makes a comprehensive presentation for all in his field, including his keenest competitors.

As a starter, Haas cites the value of an agent, on the spot in New York, to every photographer producing material that has lasting file value. He declares: "When magazines, advertising agencies, and book publishers need illustrations, they call upon the established photo services. They have neither the time nor the manpower to rout out individual photographers all round the country, who may have some of the pictures they seek. I know how slow they are to add names to their lists. Although I have operated a picture agency in New York City for twenty-one years, it is only in the last six years that the major users of pictures have called me automatically when they sought illustrations. It took fifteen years of steady selling to achieve that. So how much chance has an individual cameraman, especially if he is out of New York City, to get his share of that business?

"Very recently," Haas continues, "a steel company sent us a long list of subjects desired. It called for pictures of cities and scenes in more than a dozen countries. Because we handle the output of many photographers all over the world, we were able to fill that order completely and quickly. And many of those photographers received good royalty checks as a result of the sales to that steel company.

"From our own experience, I feel that the 50 percent royalty we deduct doesn't cost the photographer a penny. Usually we make many more sales than he would, at consistently better prices, so that his return is greater than if he made his own sales and paid no commissions. And we can do two things that the cameraman can't do for himself. First, if he shoots something of a semi-news or of a timely and therefore quickly perishable feature nature, we can show his pictures to every major market in New York within two days. It would take him much longer than that to send pictures to one place in New York and get them back. Second, if he makes pictures of a documentary or of a scenic nature, placed in our files they are readily available when we get calls for stock photographs.

"There is one exception," he goes on. "If any cameraman gets pictures of a hotel fire, earthquake, train wreck, plane crash, or other spot news, I wouldn't advise him to send such pictures to me or to anyone else in the agency field. His best bets are his local or nearby metropolitan newspapers and the major press associations. But I do want to impress one thing on all photographers lucky enough to be on the spot when news breaks. Don't sell anything but the first newspaper publication rights to either newspapers or syndicates. That is a point that is too often overlooked. If the photographer reserves the other rights, he can, either directly or indirectly through an agent, cash in on later sales to magazines, books, and any other type of publication use. I did exactly that myself when I sold the Esposito murder pictures to the New York *News*."

Though European already acts as agent for approximately two hundred photographers, ranging from amateurs to full-time professionals, it is not a closed market for the man seeking an agent. But it is a limited one. Either for royalty selling or outright purchase, picture stories, documentary, and scenic photos offered to European must meet the highest professional pictorial standards. For anything less than the best it doesn't pay European to devote time and space to the material, and the contributing photographer will be disappointed with the financial return. Though Haas makes outright purchase of semi-news singles and occasionally of picture stories, he prefers the royalty basis for feature material. As he puts it: "It is fairer to the photographer. After all, I won't buy anything for a fixed fee unless I am rather certain that I can sell it for at least twice that amount. The royalty system, I feel, is better for both of us. I'll do my best to sell pictures that I wouldn't buy outright speculatively, so the photographer gets a much wider market.

"There is something else," Haas adds. "Too many photographers send the same photographs to several agencies instead of just to one. Usually that doesn't increase sales, because most of us are selling in the same market to the same customers. And if we know our competitors are also handling a man's product, we don't push it as hard as the pictures we know are exclusive with us. As every camera fan knows, there are many gradations of gray between absolute black and white. That is true of statements like mine too. There are always exceptions. For instance, there is nothing wrong with sending the same pictures to an agency specializing in dealing with advertisers and never or hardly ever calling on magazines, and to another that never goes near an advertiser, but is in constant touch with all types of publications. But, by and large, it is best to deal exclusively with one agent.

"I know most photographers think taking 50 percent for selling pictures is a pretty soft racket," Haas continues. "But we earn our fees. Photographers don't know, or maybe they don't want to know, that we must pay office rent, salaries, maintain files of their pictures, hire messengers, and also have other expenses. We are on call by magazines and newspapers seven days a week and twenty-four hours a day. More than once I've gotten out of bed for a middle-of-the-night emergency request. And often we work far into the night checking files for pictures the client needed the day before he asked for them."

Besides selling their pictures on royalty, European calls upon regular contributors when it receives picture-story assignments. When the story is for European's own service, Haas offers a flat fee for the job. When it is on definite order from a magazine or other publication, the photographer is given 60 percent of the price paid by the customer. Of course, in such cases there are no further royalties. The story becomes the property of the publication which ordered it and all negatives are delivered to it.

Before we go on to other agencies, it might be well to heed a photographer who has tried an agent and didn't like the experience. The agency advocates make much of their ability to be on the job for the photographer where pictures are being bought. Those three words, "on the job," seem to be the crux of the matter. Our photographer friend doesn't think they are always on the job. At least one of them didn't seem to be for him.

He tried a New York agency. They held quite a collection of his picture stories for months and sold nary a one. He finally demanded their return. Then he made the rounds of the publications himself. Within a few weeks he had sold half the pictures which had been resting in the agency files for months.

Maybe his is an extreme case. Perhaps he picked a poor agency or one not too effective with his type of picture story. And he may be an exceptionally good salesman himself. Also because he lives in New York, he was in a better position to represent himself than would be a cameraman hundreds or thousands of miles away.

But he came to a conclusion which is worth passing along to every free-lance who is considering turning his pictures over to an agent. Our friend says: "When and if you decide to try one of the agencies, come to an agreement as to a trial period during which it will have exclusive rights to represent you. It can be ten days, several weeks, or a few months, but it should be for a definite period. Then, if the agency has not made any or enough sales within the trial period, you can get your pictures back, try another agency, or peddle them yourself."

Picture agencies operating on royalty are not limited to New York, though the great majority of them are in that city. Leslie Jacobi operates the well-established Publix Pictures in Chicago (11), with offices at 410 North Michigan Avenue. Jacobi deals heavily in Kodachromes for calendars, but covers other phases of picture selling as well. Probably it would be best to let him describe his own operations. He writes:

"We have been established in Chicago as photographers' agents for over ten years, and we sell to the whole of the United States as well as to South America and to Europe. We work on a commission basis, and our commission varies from 33⅓ percent to 50 percent, depending on the character of the material.

"We specialize in supplying Kodachromes for calendars, but we also serve magazines, book publishers, and other editorial and commercial users. We are interested in obtaining a few more top-flight suppliers, especially of human-interest, children, and animal Kodachromes not smaller than 4 by 5, and we also look for black-and-white features and black-and-white single prints. Above all we are interested in good magazine photographers in this and foreign countries who can execute assignments in black and white and color for our various magazine customers."

In Tucson, Arizona, Western Ways not only runs its own feature production business, but acts as sales agent for photographers. Of course, owing to its regional location, most calls to Western Ways are for pictures of the Rocky Mountain area, southwestern United States, and northwestern Mexico. So it prefers to represent photographers from these regions.

Charley Herbert, its head, has sent us a copy of the form letter that goes to cameramen who ask Western Ways to represent them. Because most agents will ask more or less the same questions, we quote part of it so that you may know what information you must supply when you seek an agent.

Herbert writes would-be contributors: "Western Ways is primarily interested in colorful, timely Western material of people, places, events, points of interest, scenic attractions, natural phenomena, industries, community activities, crafts, folklore, and novelties. We need good clear 8 by 10 glossy prints of series of pictures that tell a well-connected story in an interesting and pictorial manner.

"Color pictures, of course, bring higher prices than black-and-white, but the market for color is limited in comparison with the market for black-and-white pictures.

"Naturally, we have been able to sell Western material more readily from our location here in Tucson than material which is made in other parts of the country.

"I suggest that you send us a complete list of the material you have on hand which you feel comes up to the above requirements. It is best not to send us the material itself until we have time to go over the list and see what we think we can place best. If you care to, you could let us have one or two prints which show your technical quality for us to add to your file for future reference.

"In addition it would be helpful to us in being able to get direct assignments for you if you could give us a list of features (with details) which you could make in your territory.

"We operate on the usual agency basis of fifty-fifty of the gross amount received from any sales we make for you. If you write the article and furnish the illustrations also, you get two thirds of the gross."

With the letter Herbert encloses a form for the photographer to fill out. This is a rough copy of it.

NAME ....

last middle first

ADDRESS ....

street city (zone) state

Photo Equipment:

Transportation:

Area available to cover:

Experience:

Type of stories you like to cover: (sports, feature, news etc.)

Type of stories you are best qualified to cover:

Physical limitations:

How insured:

Will you work on free-lance (speculative basis) or only on direct assignment with all expenses paid?

Before we return to the New York agencies, we should make one thing very clear. Herbert doesn't especially stress his point about Western Ways getting best results with Rocky Mountain material; nevertheless, anyone east of the Rocky Mountain states would do better if he got an agent in New York or Chicago.

The next New York City agency on our list is PIX, Incorporated, at 250 Park Avenue, New York 17. PIX does not try to run a daily syndicate service. It is wholly a sales agent for individual cameramen. According to sales manager Franz E. Furst, its business can be divided roughly into three main groupings.

PIX's first and principal activity is getting assignments for the photographers it represents. Division of the proceeds between PIX and its cameramen varies with the nature of the job to be covered. For black-and-white picture assignments the customary division is fifty-fifty. When an assignment calls for color, the split is usually forty for the agency and sixty percent for the photographer. There are good reasons for giving the photographer more for color work. To start with, his initial investment in materials is higher. And the investment of PIX is less, because it does not have the expense of printing enlargements and other processing costs that are part of a black-and-white assignment. Since the photographer turns over completely processed color transparencies, all PIX must do is see that captions are completed and delivery is made in time to meet publication deadlines.

PIX's second field is selling complete picture stories, and occasionally single shots, for photographers who produce them on their own initiative. Furst advises that newcomers who wish PIX to represent them can submit either negatives or prints for examination when querying. In either case complete captions are necessary.

If Furst feels the submitted material is salable and the photographer decides to let PIX represent him, the normal procedure is to borrow his negatives. Usually one set of prints isn't enough. Extra sets are needed for local sales after the first-right purchaser has published the story and for air-mailing overseas for foreign sales. On these sales the photographer receives the customary fifty percent.

The third and smallest part of its business is, strangely enough, the one PIX finds most expensive to operate. It is selling pictures from the file of stock shots—personalities, scenes, documentary photographs, and so on. Although maintaining the files entails operating costs that are quite high, the photographer doesn't suffer thereby. He still gets his fifty percent royalty on sales. While the file end of the business is least profitable and sometimes is annoyingly time-consuming, PIX, like others in the same field, finds that maintaining a file is an essential service demanded by the publications with which it does business. Directly and indirectly, it helps the agency keep the close contacts with editors needed for getting special assignments and for finding a ready market for picture stories.

As part of its sales effort, PIX at frequent intervals issues a mimeographed news-letter that is sent to editors in the United

States and Canada and to the European agencies acting for the agency overseas. It carries brief listings of new feature-picture sets, noting sizes of prints or negatives, whether black-and-white or color, short descriptions of the subjects, and the name of the cameraman who made them. The news-letter also lists new portraits and fashion photographs produced by PIX photographers. Editors are kept posted on the whereabouts of traveling photographers; the news-letter tells where they are and where they will be going, with approximate dates of arrival and departure for each stopping place.

Within limits, all agencies are seeking new photographers to add to those they already represent. PIX is no exception. Furst says the outfit is always happy to hear, preferably by mail, from aspiring feature photographers. The initial letter should include a brief account of ability and practical experience, description of type and amount of equipment, and some samples of the inquirer's work (much the same information as that outlined in the Western Ways form, you will note). Usually from such a letter, Furst says, PIX can decide whether it will be profitable to pursue the matter further or sign off immediately. If you keep in mind that PIX's offerings are limited to features, picture stories, art, human interest, unusual portraiture, and the like, you will not waste your time and the agency's by writing about other types of photography. PIX does not handle spot news at all.

According to its president, Roy Lester, Graphic House, with its own sales and production offices in New York, Los Angeles, Paris, and Venice, is the largest photo agency specializing in feature material. It produces between one hundred and fifty to two hundred feature sets a month. And those sets never run below a minimum of twelve pictures and quite often run up close to a hundred or more.

Scattered around the world and directed from the New York home at 280 Madison Avenue are twenty-seven staff photographers. None is on salary; all accept instead the customary fifty-fifty split. Of course Graphic House has to provide them with enough work and sales to make it worth their while.

Surprisingly enough, this firm does very little color work. Practically its entire production is black-and-white. Also it operates photo laboratories in all its offices twenty-four hours a day, seven days a week. For that reason from both its staff photographers and its independent contributors it prefers to receive undeveloped film so every step of processing can be controlled.

Free-lances will be glad to know that it is Graphic House policy to include photographers' credit lines, though it does not always succeed in getting them carried in publications. It also does a big job of theatrical coverage. In magazines and Sunday newspapers you may have seen theatrical production photos credited to Eileen Darby—Graphic House. That is her specialty, but no longer the major portion of the firm's business, though she is Mrs. Lester.

Because in the main their operations are so similar to those already described, there is no point in making a detailed examination of other picture sales agencies. Additional New York sales outfits are:

Black Star, 420 Lexington Ave. (17)
Combine, 271 Madison Ave. (16)
F.P.G., 219 E. 44th St. (17)
Globe Photos, 139 W. 54th St. (19)
Giullemette, 425 Fifth Ave. (17)
Keystone, 21 W. 46th St. (19)
Scope and Magnum, 67 W. 44th St. (18)
Shostal Press Agency, 545 Fifth Ave. (17)
Three Lions, Inc., 545 Fifth Ave. (17)
Transatlantic News Features, 125 E. 50th St. (22)

Across the border in Canada there are three picture sales agencies: Wheeler Newspaper Syndicate, 302 Bay Street, Toronto 1, Ontario; Miller Service, Ltd., 19 Melinda Street, Toronto 1, Ontario; and Canada Wide Feature Service, Ltd., 231 St. James Street W., Montreal 1, Quebec. This last is an affiliate of the Montreal *Star* newspaper group. As to the scope of Canadian operations, we will quote Tom Wheeler, who heads the oldest syndicate in the Dominion: "All three listings operate nationally; we sell all available markets in the nation. And if any honest buck can be made abroad, fine. Usual basis: royalty."

Combine Photos, Ltd., with offices at 271 Madison Avenue, New York 16, is one of the few agencies operated by a woman, Mrs. Jack Lewis. It was started originally to represent a group of London picture agencies in the United States; it is now a wholly American-owned business in the general picture-agency field. While its policy on payment in general sticks to the usual fifty-fifty split, on assignments it reimburses the photographer for materials and expenses before dividing the remainder of the payment for the job.

Jack Lewis, who occasionally lends his wife a hand in running the business, has some definite ideas of the value of any agency to photographers. He says: "It is axiomatic that no one person can be in two places at the same time. If a photographer is covering an assignment, his mind should be there, too. He cannot afford to be distracted by wondering whether or not a specific set of pictures he may have sent off has reached the editor. An on-the-job agent, well and favorably known, can relieve him of such worries, leaving him to concentrate on photography, while the agent takes over the business end and the sales."

Among the small, independent agencies are two that cannot be classified with the others. Both, in the true sense, are markets for photographers in that they purchase pictures offered by contributors. These two are Culver Service, 205 East 42nd Street, New York 17, and Ewing Galloway, 420 Lexington Avenue, New York 17.

Culver's stock in trade is old pictures; he is not interested in anything current. He will buy outright either negatives or prints from old collections. But don't offer him anything made much later than 1900. He won't be interested.

Galloway wants more modern material, but he doesn't want news pictures. If the action and photography are striking enough, he can use accidents, fires, disasters, and the like, although he will not be interested in them until their immediate spot-news value is over. What Galloway is hunting is material that can be sold over and over again as illustrations. And he is willing to pay good prices for such negatives. He prefers outright purchase to royalty handling, though on rare occasions he may enter a royalty deal. He has compiled a list of instructions for voluntary contributors. It is much too long to reprint here but the opening statement is worth noting. Galloway says: "Every picture we buy must meet two fundamental requirements:

"1. *Superior Photography,* such as you see reproduced in well-illustrated literary periodicals, class journals, advertisements, and textbooks.

"2. *Subject Matter* that is illustrative in nature and which appeals to the publishing world, as above."

Before we close this discussion of the picture services as marketing outlets, we should mention the so-called mat services. As a practical matter they aren't much of a market. But you should know that and not waste time and money trying to break into a non-existent field.

Probably most of the news pictures published in daily and weekly newspapers reach those publications in the form of matrices (mats) rather than as photographic prints. The results are not quite as good, but the costs are very much lower. The papers pay less for a mat service than they do for a print service. And when the pictures reach the newspaper several costly operations, principally art work and making half-tone engravings, are eliminated.

Basically, in the case of three major agencies, using mats is just another means of distributing pictures. When a spot-news picture is bought by AP, Acme, and International, it may be used, if both picture and news are hot enough, on the wire, in the mail service, and on the mat pages. Only one payment is made for such triple use and only one picture is needed by the receiving agency. That holds true for the picture mats issued by the services' affiliates, NEA, in the case of Acme, and King Features for International. Neither NEA nor King Features buys spot-news pictures directly from contributors.

About the only mat service that buys news photographs is Central Press Association, at 1435 East 12th Street, Cleveland 14, Ohio. It produces several pages of matted spot-news and feature pictures every day in Cleveland in addition to the mats put out by its New York, Chicago, and San Francisco bureaus.

Its managing editor, Courtland C. Smith, says: "Although Central Press receives the great majority of its photographs through its affiliate, International News Photos, it also buys considerable numbers of pictures from correspondents and free-lances. These are principally of a feature nature, although it will consider spot-news pictures if they can be obtained speedily.

"In the feature-picture category, Central Press also uses photo lay-outs, consisting of three to five photographs telling a picture story. These should be accompanied by plenty of caption material to supply the editors with all information that might be needed for a very brief story as well as the lines for the individual photos.

"A reminder might be in order that, since Central Press is a news organization, accuracy of information accompanying all material is particularly important."

Two concerns issue full-page feature mats for which they buy sets of photographs occasionally, but so very occasionally that we wouldn't recommend that anyone try to crack them. The odds are much too long against the contributor. And neither one has been successful in finding regular contributors who can meet their strict pictorial and editorial standards.

One of these full-page feature mats, issued once a week by AP Newsfeatures, is Picture Show. Each page is a unit telling a complete story in pictures and text. The pictures must carry the burden of the tale, with words restricted to a brief general account and cut-lines for the individual pictures. Most of AP's subscribers get the mats, though a few receive separate photographic prints with a page proof for text and as a guide to picture lay-out. Of the 52 lay-outs issued each year, probably not more than four or five come from contributors.

King Features puts out the other full-page mats telling a single story. Two of King's Picture Page are mailed to subscribers each week. That's twice as many as Picture Show, but the chances of selling a set are no better. In the course of a year perhaps ten sets are bought. And then the sellers are likely to be established agencies selling professionally produced lay-outs. The opportunity for the lone free-lance here is mighty slim.

All the other lay-outs for Picture Page result from assignments made by the editors to staff photographers or to full-time professional feature cameramen. The editors furnish the basic concepts. After the idea is evolved, picture development is discussed and then the form of the lay-out is set down in words as a complete shooting script. Basically, though it uses fewer pictures, the task is the same as producing a feature series for a magazine. And the procedures are much the same as those described in the chapters on feature photography. Often in addition to verbal descriptions, the Picture Page editors include sketches in shooting scripts, usually to show position, size, and angles needed for particular photo shots.

The editorial requirements for Picture Page are exceedingly high. The subject must be either newsy, popular science, or of great human interest. The story must have a message that is interesting to practically everyone. Not only must the theme rate full-page treatment, but the pictures themselves must be dramatic, outstanding photographs.

We repeat, both Picture Show and Picture Page are the toughest of markets to crack. We think every photographer can use his time much more profitably cultivating fields where there is a better chance of harvesting a paying crop. But if you regard tough markets as a challenge and you enjoy butting your head against stone walls, here's how to communicate with the two. For Picture Show, it is best to submit your query or your pictures through the AP bureau nearest to you. If that happens to be New York City, then address the Editor, AP Newsfeatures, 50 Rockefeller Plaza, New York 20, N.Y. For Picture Page, your query (write, don't call in person or telephone) should be addressed to the Executive Editor, King Features Syndicate, 235 East 45th Street, New York 17, N.Y.

As closing advice, a word on color. The smaller agencies, as we have pointed out, handle color because there is a magazine market for transparencies. But neither the spot-news print services nor the mat services want color. This also holds for features in the cases of the big fellows, Acme, International, Wide World, and Metro, which make outright purchases for distribution to their newspaper members or subscribers. However, the color field is growing, and some day there may be a syndicate market for it. Wire transmission of color is the subject of much study and experimentation. Many newspaper Sunday magazine and rotogravure picture sections now use color. But they buy it direct or produce it themselves. For the free-lance that is an advantage; he has a wider market than he would have if the big picture services were in the field.

What the Newspapers Want

THERE IS NO GETTING AWAY from it. If you like the thrill of making spot-news pictures and seeing those photographs published, you must study your local newspaper. It can be a country weekly, a small-town daily, or a big sheet in a big metropolitan center. Become familiar with its picture requirements and find out which editors make picture assignments and which pass upon photographs submitted for publication.

Your local newspaper is more than just a potential market in itself. Its pictorial wants are also an excellent guide to the needs of the national picture-distributing agencies. That isn't at all difficult to understand. After all, the daily newspapers and, to some extent, the weeklies are the customers or clients of the picture syndicates. Naturally, the syndicates try to obtain and deliver to their clients the type of news pictures they want. Conversely local newspapers, large and small, often look to the press associations to guide them in evaluating news-picture values.

Of course, defining just what those values are is not simple. In dealing with news, even in pictorial form, we are dealing with intangibles. News isn't a measurable or standardized item like a loaf of bread or a pound of sugar. But basically it is anything that is new and of interest to a great many people.

Don't let this blind you to the fact that there are vast differences between individual newspapers inside the general pattern. The picture requirements of the sedate New York *Times,* for instance, are in many respects quite different from those of the lively New York *News.* But you may be surprised to learn how often both will use the identical picture from a press association. Such papers may show wide divergence on coverage of crime, accident, and other local and national news, but in fields like politics, foreign affairs, war, and sports, editorial reactions to photographs are surprisingly consistent over the whole newspaper field.

Depending upon where you live, you read either a local daily or one printed in the nearest metropolitan city. If you go over it carefully, you will become well acquainted with the type of photographs it uses. The credit lines will tell how much, if any, of its picture budget is produced by staff photographers and free-lance local photographers, and how much comes from one or more of the national picture services. If you don't already know, a letter of inquiry is an easy way to find out whether the editors of your paper (1) encourage contributors who are lucky enough to make spot-news pictures, (2) do not actively solicit but welcome the cameraman who phones or comes in with usable material, or (3) discourage contributors altogether. This last is rare; editors for the most part welcome the man who drops a swell news picture onto their desks.

In person and by mail we queried a number of representative newspapers to ascertain their attitude toward voluntary contributions. The responses might show, first, whether there is a trend or fairly consistent nation-wide policy on contributions; second, from them we could pass along to you first-hand information on the requirements of some of the publications that do welcome voluntary news-picture contributions.

As might be expected, the keenest in the quest for spot-news pictures are the tabloids, with their emphasis on picture journalism, and such full-size dailies as those in the Hearst chain, which feature rather complete photographic coverage of the news. New York City has three prime examples—the tabloid New York *News*, the tabloid New York *Mirror*, and the full-size New York *Journal-American*, the latter two both Hearst-owned. They not only encourage free-lance contributors but actively compete for the pictures the free-lances may produce.

For example, every time a lucky photographer-on-the-spot breaks into the New York *News* with a picture of a fire, an accident, or other spontaneous newsworthy happening, that paper calls the feat to the attention of other camera fans. It usually prints a box something like this:

FIRE PAYS ON HIS PIX

Spencer McCoy got a pay-off from his hobby yesterday. McCoy, who lives at 136 E. 36th St., heard the clang of fire engines and dashed out of his house with his camera.

The blaze was across the street in the old Amherst Club at Lexington Ave. and 36th St. He snapped several pictures and brought them to the *News*. One is in today's centerfold. You, too, can turn your hobby into cash, for the *News* pays handsomely for newsworthy shots. Call the City Desk of the *News*, Mu 2-1234, or bring your undeveloped negatives to the City Editor of the *News*, 220 E. 42nd St.

With variations to suit their own particular requirements, the *Mirror* and the *Journal-American* often run the same sort of come-on. And the other fourteen of the sixteen Hearst newspapers in the United States intensively cultivate the amateur and free-lance fields in their territories.

Quotations from some letters written by Dick Sarno, photo director of the Hearst newspapers, to the managing editors of those papers shows how highly the Hearst chain values amateur contributions and what it is doing to encourage them. In one such general letter to editors, he wrote:

"As you know, some of our papers have been very successful in receiving some good material from the amateurs and free-lances. On the other hand, some have not been too successful—perhaps due to the fact that they have not been sufficiently encouraging to the amateurs. In talking to several amateur photographic clubs around the country, some of them have clearly stated that the reason they do not return to the papers with an excellent news shot after the first try is because of the treatment received in some of the photographic labs. They point out that they are treated as though they were in the way.

"In the future perhaps we can go all out and give the so-called Johnny-on-the-spot amateurs and free-lance photographers the full treatment in the way of encouragement, patience, courtesy, etc. We cannot sell the amateur photographer too short. It is possible that he may come up with the prize picture of the year."

As Sarno remarks, although there has been much improvement in cameras, lenses, flash bulbs, film and picture-transmission methods, no one has yet invented a way of making a photograph of an event without being there with a camera. Thus, although the sixteen Hearst papers in the United States have about 250 staff photographers, the amateurs often come up with the best spot-news pictures.

Sarno, who is a veteran newspaper staff cameraman and was a top photographic instructor and combat photographer as a Signal Corps captain in World War II, points up the importance of the amateur on the spot by recalling one of his own assignments in the early thirties. He was then a staff photographer on the New York *Mirror*. He was in the office when a flash came in about an accident on lower Avenue A.

A large truck had hit a private car, sprawling its four occupants over the pavement. Three died instantly and an ambulance took the fourth to a hospital. Although he rushed to the scene, by the time he got there, the police had cleaned up the wreckage and removed the bodies and injured. There was nothing for him to photograph except a damaged automobile at the curb.

Luckily a bystander told him that the corner druggist had dashed out, the second person on the scene, and made pictures. So Sarno went to see him. Yes, he had made pictures. When he heard the crash of colliding cars he had picked up one of the $1.50 Brownies in his stock, slipped in a roll of 19¢ film, and shot the scene.

Sarno offered to buy the camera. The druggist said that wasn't necessary; he would remove the film and take the retail price of 19¢. He had not thought of doing anything with the roll except developing the couple of exposures for his own album. Then Sarno mentioned publication; the druggist was interested but still unconcerned about money returns. Sarno finally forced $20 on the reluctant photographer and rushed back to the *Mirror*. The pictures were good, so good that the *Journal-American* and International Newsphotos also used them, Sarno recollects, and paid the druggist another $50.

Preoccupation with the spot-news product of amateur photographers is not a new development for the Hearst papers. A letter, dated July 10, 1946, from Dick Sarno to all the managing editors, proves that. He wrote:

> Enclosed is one of the best spot-news photographs, made by an *AMATEUR,* that has ever appeared in a newspaper. This exceptionally fine shot was printed in the New York *Mirror,* Tuesday, July 9. It is a dramatic picture of a man about to die, slipping off the parapet on the 85th floor of the Empire State Building. Captioned "At the Brink of Eternity," this shot was taken by amateur J. Royce Ellington, who used a pocket-size B-2 Agfa camera while he was in the Observation Tower of the Empire State Building. The *Mirror* ran a by-line, of course. This is one to attract the interest of thousands of amateurs throughout the country.
>
> There are approximately 15,000 former GI photographers in the United States who have Leicas, Contax, and other types of cameras strapped around their necks. Also, at a recent photographic manufacturers' convention in Buffalo, it was pointed out that according to the record of sales, every third person in America has a camera of some type. All of these amateur photographers are constantly on the look-out for candid spot-news shots, and such coverage carries tremendous possibilities for action pictures beyond the scope of our own photographers.
>
> This would indicate that there is little chance of any important event being unphotographed regardless of where or when it might occur.
>
> I believe that it would be beneficial for our papers to take advantage of this condition, and suggest that our papers might offer prizes, which do not have to be large, for spot-news or feature pictures taken and submitted by amateurs.
>
> I realize that some of our papers have already offered prizes for photographs of this nature taken by amateurs, but I believe the enclosed picture will inspire additional valuable contributions. It should be emphasized to these amateurs that much of the value of their spot-news shots depends upon the speed with which they submit pictures to your paper.
>
> (*signed*) RICHARD L. SARNO

We asked Sarno for advice to aspiring amateurs who wish to

make news pictures. "Keep your camera with you at all times," was his immediate rejoinder, and he added: "If you travel by automobile, keep it in the glove compartment or some other safe place. It should be out of sight to avoid tempting sneak thieves, but handy enough to be readily available. And always keep it loaded, ready for action."

That suggestion can be followed with profit by every photographer, including professional full-time staff cameramen. It's a long-shot operation to be sure, but just imagine how any photographer would feel if he ran smack into a big story and didn't have his camera with him.

As to types of cameras, Sarno refuses to express a preference. He points out that the Empire State Building suicide photo was made with an old, inexpensive outfit. He feels it is much better to be on the scene with a $2 camera than to be a couple of miles away with thousands of dollars' worth of the latest in photographic gear. The main thing is to have a camera in good operating condition, to have it loaded, and to know how to operate it so that you get a picture every time.

With minor local variations, each of the sixteen Hearst newspapers regularly prints an appeal for spot-news pictures. This one, from the New York *Journal-American,* is typical.

GET CASH FOR PHOTOS

> The *Journal-American* pays liberally for spot-news photos. If you're lucky enough to be on the scene with your camera when big things happen, shoot away, then phone the City Editor at Courtlandt 7-1212. If he's interested in what you have he'll tell you to rush your undeveloped film to him at 220 South St., Manhattan.
>
> Remember, SPEED COUNTS.

Besides the strictly news and feature photo openings, the Hearst papers provide other opportunities for the amateur. Some members of the chain have run various types of camera contests for amateurs. One in the Chicago *Herald-American* drew 5,719 snapshots in a single month. Another in the New York *Journal-*

American offered a weekly prize of $25 for the best photographs in a "This Is New York" contest.

Before leaving the Hearst newspapers, we should reprint the general appeal that the whole chain has issued to amateur and free-lance photographers. Here it is:

A-T-T-E-N-T-I-O-N

ADVANCED AMATEURS AND FREE-LANCERS

Liberal pay for exclusive SPOT NEWS, FEATURES, and HUMAN INTEREST pictures if accepted for publication.

Rush NEGATIVES or PHOTOS to Picture Editor of the nearest Hearst Newspaper (see list below) or to the International News Photo representative in your REGION.

HEARST NEWSPAPERS

Albany *Times-Union*
Baltimore *News-Post*
Boston *American*
Boston *Record-American*
Chicago *Herald-American*
Detroit *Times*
Los Angeles *Examiner*
Los Angeles *Herald-Express*
Milwaukee *Sentinel*
New York *Journal-American*
New York *Mirror*
Pittsburgh *Sun-Telegraph*
San Antonio *Light*
San Francisco *Call-Bulletin*
San Francisco *Examiner*
Seattle *Post-Intelligencer*

INTERNATIONAL NEWS PHOTOS
(Gen'l Headquarters: 235 East 45 Street, New York 19)

REMEMBER — S-P-E-E-D — COUNTS!

Another large chain, the eighteen Scripps-Howard papers, also is glad to see any amateur, or professional too, for that matter, who shows up with a good picture of a spot-news event. Unlike the Hearst chain, Scripps papers don't actively seek contributions, but they always welcome voluntary contributions. Speed counts there too, of course, so any Scripps-Howard paper will gladly develop films and pay liberally for any accepted photographs. And pictures published in the Scripps-Howard newspapers have a high rate of pickup by Acme Newspictures, an affiliate. That means extra payment for the contributing photographer.

The Scripps-Howard newspapers are listed below so you may determine which is nearest to you and would therefore be a good market when and if you and spot news are at the same place at the same time.

Albuquerque *Tribune,* Albuquerque, New Mexico
Birmingham *Post-Herald,* 1531 3rd Ave. N., Birmingham 2, Ala.
Cincinnati *Post,* Post Sq. and Elm St., Cincinnati 2, Ohio
Cleveland *Press,* E. 9th St. and Rockwell Ave., Cleveland 14, Ohio
Columbus *Citizen,* 34 N. 3rd St., Columbus 15, Ohio
Denver *Rocky Mountain News,* 1720 Walton St., Denver 2, Colorado
El Paso *Herald-Post,* Mills and Kansas Sts., El Paso, Texas
Evansville *Press,* 201 N. W. 2nd St., Evansville 3, Ind.
Fort Worth *Press,* Fort Worth 1, Texas.
Houston *Press,* Rusk and Chartres Sts., Houston 1, Texas
Indianapolis *Times,* 214 W. Maryland St., Indianapolis 9, Ind.
Knoxville *News-Sentinel,* 208 W. Church Ave., Knoxville 10, Tenn.
Memphis *Commercial-Appeal,* Memphis 1, Tenn.
Memphis *Press-Scimitar,* Memphis 1, Tenn.
New York *World-Telegram and Sun,* 125 Barclay St., New York 15, N.Y.
Pittsburgh *Press,* Blvd. of the Allies, Pittsburgh 30, Pa.
San Francisco *News,* 812 Mission St., San Francisco 1, Cal.
Washington *News,* 1013 13th St., N. W., Washington 5, D.C.

Now let us leave the chains and study the attitudes of individual newspapers to picture contributors. Because they make the strongest competitive effort for the favor of the amateur and free-lance semi-professional and professional cameramen, we should turn first to the three New York City newspapers that go all out for spot-news picture contributions.

The New York *News* has not kept a separate file of pictures submitted by amateurs. Some that stand out in the memories of the editors are the famous slanting deck shot of the sinking *Vestris* in 1928, a plane crash on a holiday week-end at La Guardia Field, and in 1950 the fatal Long Island Rail Road collision at Rockville Center and the munitions explosion at Perth Amboy, New Jersey.

The *News* holds the door open for such contributions, both for its daily issues and its Sunday *News* Coloroto Section. That isn't an innovation. The paper has always been most encouraging to the photographers lucky enough to make a good spot-news picture. But, according to George Schmidt, photo assignment editor, the tempo has been stepped up in the last five or six years. As World War II entered its final phases and the quantity of pictures from the war areas decreased, the effort to procure more domestic and local photographs increased.

Here are some things to remember when and if you get a spot-news shot that, you think, may be right for the New York *News*. Its editors don't want photographers rushing into the office unannounced. They prefer that cameramen telephone first. From long experience the men on the picture assignment desk can pretty well determine from a telephoned description whether a shot has enough chance of being published to make it worthwhile for the photographer to rush his undeveloped film to the *News* office.

According to Schmidt, the *News* gets an average of 100 telephoned picture inquiries weekly. Occasionally someone wanders in with undeveloped film without telephoning first. The 100 weekly queries are winnowed down to about 30 or 40 requests to "bring in your pictures." And of these about three or four get used. That makes the batting average of free-lance spot-news contributors about .040. Four percent is a very low rate of acceptance, which simply points up again the jackpot or sweepstake odds against selling spot-news pictures.

Actually a contributor dealing with the *News* makes a bit more from his spot-news efforts than these figures would indicate. Close to 40 percent of those who telephone get some reward. For once the *News* assignment editors tell a cameraman to bring in his film, he is certain to receive some payment. Even if the picture isn't used, the photographer is given a messenger fee that is more than enough to cover fares to the *News* office, replacement cost of film and bulbs, and something for his time and trouble. He misses the thrill of seeing his picture in print and getting a big check, but at least he gets back a few dollars and free processing of his films.

If his photograph gets into the *News*, then the contributor does very well. There are no set fees and to prevent comparisons—every contributing photographer thinks his pictures outshine all others—the *News* will not disclose its prices. It judges each picture on its own merits, basing its prices on several factors. These include the page of the paper on which the picture is printed, the size of the reproduction, and the news value of the story. To the total for these is added an incentive amount to encourage the photographer to keep looking for spot-news shots and to bring his pictures to the *News*.

The incentive pay system, giving photographers a bit more than the strict yardstick of values indicates, has worked out well. The *News* has found that through the years it has thus built up a little band of regular and consistent contributors. Some come through with a picture submission weekly; others make almost daily telephone inquiries. And they click often enough to make their enterprise pay good dividends.

Schmidt reports that among the pictures offered are occasional oddities or very interesting feature-type shots a little bit removed from the regular run of spot news. But leading the procession week in and week out, auto accidents are in first place. Pictures of fires are a close second. That means the free-lance must work exceedingly fast. The *News* itself gets immediate reports of every accident and every fire. And it is very quick to rush out its staff cameramen, not only from the main office but from strategic bases nearer the news scene.

Though 99 times out of every 100 speed is essential, once in a great while a graphic photograph of a train wreck, auto accident, fire, and the like, may be used even though the pictures arrive a day or two late. While that doesn't mean that you should linger in submitting pictures, it does mean that you shouldn't give up altogether if circumstances keep you from getting in immediate touch with newspaper markets. If you have a striking exclusive picture, don't let a delay of as much as a day keep you from trying to sell it.

On occasion, the *News* has been delighted to receive such tardy offerings. Camera-carrying tourists driving to New York often run smack into good opportunities for news pictures. Should you do this, telephone from where you are, and, if encouraged, rush the film where and how directed. But vacationers usually feel the trip comes first and put off efforts to market pictures until they reach their destination.

Such photographers may still have a chance to sell their pictures. But if the *News* is their market, they must first hurdle a couple of big "ifs." The first "if" is exclusivity. If the story hasn't been covered photographically by anyone else, chances are higher. And second, even if others have covered it but have made mediocre pictures which were not used by competing newspapers or distributed by the picture agencies, the *News* may be interested if the picture submitted is particularly outstanding. The *News* has bought photographs under such circumstances before and probably will do so again.

Another type of photo also may be salable days after the event: pictures of disasters or rescues at sea taken by passengers and crew members. They are less common now than when ships were the only means of crossing the ocean and, when the accident occurs close enough to shore, they have been supplanted to some extent by air views. However, shipboard pictures will retain prime news values until the vessels reach port or, sometimes these days, until they are met by planes carrying reporters and photographers as they near the coast.

Normally photographers who get such shots find it unnecessary to query the newspapers or press associations. Instead they wait until the newsmen board the ship at quarantine and hold out for their highest offers. There will be spirited bidding. It will also be hurried, because the pictures must be speeded back to offices to catch editions.

However, radioing a query ahead or using ship-to-shore telephone may be a good idea for a photographer acquainted with possible markets. If you have sold to that market before, the editors may have enough confidence in you to make a definite radio bid. In any case, if the story is big enough it will speed up things both for you and for the newspaper or press association with which you deal. Its representatives will come to you first on boarding the ship.

Here is another tip on marketing pictures made at sea. Check the captain, purser, and radio operator to learn whether they have received shore queries about photographs. If the story is hot enough, both newspapers and press associations will be using the ship-to-shore phone to find out whether pictures have been made and, if so, to bid for them before the ship reaches port. There is nothing new in that procedure; newspapers have been doing that ever since the invention of wireless.

To return to the *News,* that paper buys pictures for its Sunday Coloroto Section that are very definitely not spot news. Here speed is not so important, but delay isn't encouraged. The fresher the photographs the better their chances of acceptance. Wanted material includes all kinds of exclusive feature-picture stories and single shots that tell a story. These can be submitted either in color or in black and white. In most cases the *News* prefers to center its picture stories around people; it also regularly runs an Animal Corner; and on some occasions it uses interesting and eye-catching shots of scenics, industrial and scientific subjects, and so on.

The *News* emphasizes that both for daily spot-news pictures and Sunday feature pictures, caption material is important. The editors write: "We want complete, extensive text material for our picture stories. We want quotes and opinions of the people pictured. We want dates, names, places, ages, dimensions, etc. GOOD STORIES MAY BE REJECTED FOR LACK OF CAPTION MATERIAL.

"For the Coloroto Section," they continue, "print quality must be top-notch. We cannot use muddy, careless, overly dark, or flat prints. They should have snap and sparkle. In case of doubt, contributors should include negatives with any prints submitted. They will be returned. GOOD STORIES MAY BE REJECTED FOR LACK OF GOOD PRINTS.

"Generally, we do not care for 'contrived' stories—that is, picture situations that have a posed or phony ring. If certain situations demand posed characters, pose them in natural and non-static positions.

"Lighting is important. Don't be afraid to use bulbs, extension cords, tripods. Make plenty of exposures. Give the picture editor an opportunity to edit. Composition is important. Cropping is important. The scene-setting shot for a story is important."

These instructions sum up the general outlines drawn in the chapters on features and caption writing. They can be followed with profit whenever you offer pictures for sale. But don't slight the Sunday *News* as a market for pictures. Payment for either a single picture or a complete lay-out is high. Both for black and white and for color the rates are about on a level with those paid by magazines for comparable material.

An equally good field for the independent photographer is the New York *Mirror*. Besides the boxes in every edition encouraging amateurs to send in pictures, it has compiled a four-page illustrated folder for non-staff photographers. It is 3½ by 6¾ inches, small enough to fit in a pocket or wallet.

Titled TAKE THAT PICTURE, with a cover-page script line adding "and speed it to the *Mirror*," the little pamphlet offers concise instructions on making and marketing pictures if sales to the *Mirror* are the ultimate goal. Here again are suggestions that might well be applied to marketing pictures to newspapers everywhere.

Some pertinent quotations follow: "While the *Mirror's* staff photographers cover acres of ground, they cannot be everywhere at the right moment. So the *Mirror* encourages amateur photographers to take pictures that tell a story wherever and whenever they can, and pays well for those accepted.

"Just assume that you are on assignment for the *Mirror*, and when you are at the scene of an event of news importance and have your camera with you, TAKE THAT PICTURE. Get the best pictures you can—first a close-up, then a semi-close-up, and finally a general scene. Rush the undeveloped negatives to the *Mirror* Picture Editor at the *Mirror* office for publication. Any size negative, or any type of camera, will do the trick."

The back of the little book tells where to bring negatives and how to phone in a query or a tip. For the *Mirror* will also pay for tips that result in pictures taken by its own photographers.

The *Mirror* does not go too far afield in its search for contributed photographs. Roughly the tri-state area of metropolitan New York City and nearby New Jersey and Connecticut receive the most intensive cultivation. Occasionally it will buy from farther away, but not very often, and then the story and pictures must be very, very good.

Like its competitors for the unplanned and unforeseen in news pictures, the *Mirror* is always happy to see the traveling amateur who on his trip may have stumbled into something good picture-wise. It is a keen bidder for pictures of maritime disasters when the ships that participate in an accident or rescue reach port. Though once in a great while the *Mirror* will print a feature-type picture made by an amateur, its quest is primarily for spot news. On a light news day a feature picture may slide through or such a photograph will be bought to encourage an amateur or other free-lance who shows promise of becoming a steady contributor.

Also like its rivals, the *Mirror* prefers to receive undeveloped film. The reason is the same—speed in getting the picture into the next edition. It prefers, too, that a telephone query precede a trip to the office with pictures. A brief description by telephone will indicate whether story and pictures have *Mirror* publication possibilities. That method is profitable for the contributing photographer. If after a telephone talk, he is told to bring in his film, he is certain, at the very least, of payment for his time, his materials, and his transportation to the *Mirror* office.

Sometimes an amateur with an inexpensive camera hits a mighty big *Mirror* jackpot. Tops, in the opinion of John Reidy, *Mirror* picture assignment editor, is the Empire State suicide photograph alluded to earlier in this chapter. It was taken by J. Royce Ellington, of Winston-Salem, North Carolina. Carrying a second-hand camera that he had bought for $10, Ellington was on the observation platform of the big New York building when a man climbed over the parapet and jumped. He landed on a ledge a few stories lower down. Then while Ellington and other sightseers urged him to stop, he crawled over the edge of the roof. Shooting almost straight down, Ellington caught the suicide as his fingers clung to the parapet edge an instant before he let go to plunge to his death.

In the photograph the location was unmistakable because the shadow of the world's tallest building was etched by the sun against the lower buildings in the background. And because the camera was old and the shutter slow, the picture was slightly moved, which added much to its effectiveness.

Ellington received from the *Mirror* many times the price of his camera. International News Photos picked it up for world-wide distribution, bringing him an additional reward. Finally it won him a $50 prize in a Graflex competition.

But that is not all the story. Call it luck or what you will, sometimes a photographer can do almost everything wrong and still come out on top. As it happens Ellington broke all the rules about speed in submitting spot-news pictures.

The picture was made on a Sunday. Ellington didn't telephone the *Mirror* until Monday evening. John Reidy, who happened to be on the desk that night, answered the call. Wasting no time then, Reidy told Ellington to rush right up with the picture. Afterward Reidy asked Ellington why he waited more than twenty-four hours after the event. The North Carolinian explained that he wasn't certain he had caught the picture. So he took his film to the nearest drugstore and left it to be developed. When he picked up negatives and prints the next night and found that he had something, he finally telephoned the *Mirror*. The picture was so good that, in spite of its lateness, it caught some editions of the Tuesday-morning *Mirror* and the early editions on Wednesday.

While for its daily editions it wants spot news, the *Mirror*'s Sunday Magazine is an excellent customer for feature photographs. The payment for both color and black-and-white pictures is very good. John Walter, art editor of the *Sunday Mirror* Magazine, gives this general outline of what is wanted.

"It is very difficult," he writes, "for me to say anything but the usual thing about the features we like to use in our magazine. It may sound corny, but I still think the features we want are features with human interest.

"As far as how we would like to encourage free-lance and

amateur contributors, I would say that we have always considered any feature on its merit. We do buy black-and-white and color features, and I am speaking for myself when I say that I think in every case where we use an outside feature, we have to send for the original negatives. I like to see the full print, and crop the picture myself. This gives me a latitude in making a variety of lay-outs for our magazine."

A careful reading of the *Mirror* magazine tells us a bit more about its likes and dislikes. For one thing, there is no geographical limit to the material used. Photographer-writer teams of staff men have made long journeys to produce feature lay-outs. Among them we recall an assignment to Rome for the Holy Year ceremonies and to the Far East during the Korean fighting. While naturally such staff assignments limit the need for outside purchases, they never completely bar the photographer who can submit something original in concept and outstanding as pictorial photography.

So much for the tabloids. Now for a full-sized New York newspaper. According to Robert F. (Bob) Keogh, assignment editor of the New York *Journal-American,* his paper has been actively encouraging amateur contributors longer than any other in New York City. That is not too hard to believe, since the *Journal-American* is much older than either the *News* or the *Mirror.* Its encouragement may even antedate that of any other paper in the United States. The policy was set long before Keogh was promoted from staff photographer to assignment editor in 1926.

The *Journal-American* uses three full pages of news pictures every day of the week. Other photographs illustrating news stories are scattered through editions to break up solid type on the non-picture pages. Because it is full size, the *J - A* has room for many more photographs than a tabloid. That in turn makes it a wider market for amateur offerings.

Like its two competitors for spot-news pictures, the *Journal-American* wants would-be contributors to query by telephone before coming to the office with photos or films. Quite often, if the story is hot, the volunteer contributor will be asked to bring in his undeveloped film, even though staff photographers have been sent on the same assignment.

Keogh says there is a double reason for that policy. First, there is always a chance that the amateur on the scene at the start may have caught an angle that the staff photographer arriving later couldn't photograph. And second, because he was there sooner, the free-lance photographer may well reach the office before the staff photographer has completed his assignment at the scene. That means a time saving, and with the last edition of the *Journal-American* going to press not too late in the afternoon every minute saved is of major importance. It might mean the difference between catching or missing the edition most New Yorkers read on their way home. If the photo catches that edition, the *Journal-American* beats the next morning's papers with the pictures. If it misses, the *J - A* must either follow the morning papers the next day or skip the pictures altogether. The amateur or other free-lance who helps get a spot-news picture into print along with the story will find that he gets a better price for his photographs.

Whether or not a picture is used, the *Journal-American* follows the more or less standard practice of paying something to everyone asked to bring pictures or undeveloped films to the office. The amount will at least be enough to reimburse the camera enthusiast for time, materials, and bus or taxi fare. When a picture is used, the payment is based on a number of factors, of which news value is the most important. There is always a plus added, representing whatever sum the editors think will encourage the contributor to continue to think of the *Journal-American* first whenever he gets a good shot.

Through the years that Keogh has been encouraging amateur photographers, he has found that taxi-drivers lead all others as spot-news picture contributors. Among them are many who regularly break into the columns of his paper. He has also found that the amateur in general is not only an excellent photographic technician, but has an abundance of photographic gear.

Most of the amateurs, he discovered, have expensive and rather complete 35-millimeter (minicam) cameras and accessories. Outfits like that are fine for the photographer, but for lab-production reasons Keogh, like most newspaper photo editors, prefers larger cameras and therefore larger negative sizes. He explains: For the amateur who is never without his camera, the minicam sizes are most convenient. They are compact, hence easy to carry around and handle. Small cameras are also more economical to operate. Rolls of film are cheaper. So are auxiliary lenses, filters, and most other attachments.

But they have a drawback. For best reproduction results in newspapers and other media, 35-millimeter film requires fine-grain development. That is a slow process. And it can be a considerable handicap in spot-news picture coverage for newspapers. When edition time gets close, there isn't time for the slow lab processing 35-millimeter film requires. So either editions are missed or the lab hurries, with the result that much of the photographic quality may be lost. The newspapers won't refuse the smallest negatives, but, as we said at the start, they prefer larger sizes for speedy handling both in development and in printing enlargements for reproduction.

Next in number, Keogh has found, but far behind the minicam enthusiasts, are the amateurs and other free-lances who carry cameras using No. 120 (2¼ by 2¼) film. That is better for lab processing but not nearly so good as the 4 by 5 inch roll or cut film which fewer use, or the very rare but exceedingly welcome 5 by 7 size. Occasionally some contributor with a really old camera will submit a roll of postcard size film. Keogh reports with some surprise that he has found that many amateur camera hobbyists work with graphic cameras fully equipped with wide angle and long lenses, multiple flash devices, and other accessories that represent investments of considerably over a thousand dollars.

Although the *Journal-American* is a New York City newspaper, it doesn't limit its acceptances to contributors from its immediate territory. Keogh says the editors will be glad to receive telegraphic inquiries on hot picture stories from anywhere in the United States. If the story is hot enough and the picture possibilities seem striking enough, the free-lance contributor will be instructed to take his pictures, negatives, or prints, as the case may be, to the nearest International Soundphoto or AP Wirephoto bureau for special wire transmission to New York.

Journal-American encouragement of amateurs and other free-lance operators has gone beyond seeing that they are well received and paid liberally. Keogh puts it this way: "We not only want to get pictures for the *Journal-American,* but we want to protect the photographer's interests at all times." Normally that is done by buying only first publication rights. This permits the photographer to cash in separately on sales to photo services, magazines, house organs, and the like. And when International News Photos wants to pick up *Journal-American* pictures suitable for syndicate distribution, it must make its own deal with the contributing photographer.

When Keogh broke in as a staff photographer, he recalls that it was common practice to permit a number of free-lance cameramen to make the paper's photo lab their headquarters. And when all the staff photographers were busy, assignments were given those free-lances. For a variety of reasons that system didn't work out too well. After a few years' trial it was abolished.

Nowadays the *Journal-American* uses a modification of that method. Besides the full-time salaried staff, it hires a group of stringer photographers on a retainer basis. For being available, these men receive a minimum weekly sum and are paid an additional fee for every assignment covered. Such men are in line for full-time jobs on the photographic staff when vacancies occur. In turn stringers are recruited from among the repeater free-lance contributors.

If an amateur or semi-professional becomes a *Journal-American* repeater—that is, if he is one of the lucky individuals who is frequently Johnny-on-the-spot when picture news breaks and he sells his photographs to the *Journal-American* regularly—Keogh keeps an eye on him. If he continues to develop picture news sense, showing improvement both in composition and other techniques as well as enterprise in getting around to news breaks, he may be offered a stringer-retainer status. Then if news photography as a profession is his goal, he is well on his way to achieving that ambition.

In reminiscing his experiences with amateurs, Keogh recalled an incident that not only provided a bonanza for the lucky lady camera fan, but also gave the paper a clean beat, at the same time saving Bob a few gray hairs.

Late one afternoon in the summer of 1949, the ferry terminal on Staten Island caught fire and was completely destroyed. Though last-edition press time was almost at hand when news of the fire broke, photographers were rushed to the scene by air and boat, in the hope that at least one of them would be able to get a quick shot and rush it back to the office before the presses started rolling.

Then, as Keogh waited anxiously beside the telephone for some word from his staffers, the bell started ringing. A woman's voice came over the line. She said she was telephoning from the terminal at South Ferry. She had just come from Staten Island, and reported that as her ferryboat pulled out of the slip, there was a great burst of flame and smoke from the Staten Island ferryhouse. She had made some pictures with an old box Brownie. Would the *Journal-American* be interested? Keogh was doubtful of usable pictures, but he was desperate. So he told her to get a taxi and rush to the *Journal-American* office.

The result was a smash shot that caught the last edition and beat all the other papers. Fixed-focus Brownies and similar box cameras often produce exceedingly good pictures at infinity. And the lady, who had traveled from Colorado with her daughter for a vacation in New York City, received a check from the *Journal-American* that was more than enough to pay the entire cost of their trip.

These, then, are the best newspaper markets in New York—the *Daily News*, the *Mirror*, and the *Journal-American*. The other New York papers do not make the same intensive effort to get spot-news coverage. While none will turn down a good picture that fits into its editorial requirements, the wise seller will naturally first try the more receptive markets. For after all, the publications actively seeking spot-news picture contributions will be apt to pay higher prices than those with a "we can take it or leave it" attitude.

Before leaving New York, we should mention one more newspaper market—the Sunday Department of the New York *Times*. It is interested in features rather than spot news, and buys comparatively little from outside contributors, but when it does make a purchase the rates are good. A check on the *Times* Sunday

Magazine Section will show that it runs a varying number of picture lay-outs each week. Some, like fashions and theater, offer almost no opportunity for the contributing photographers. However, for other features the *Times* not only welcomes free-lance contributions but is happy to receive queries about picture-lay-out ideas. Invariably when an idea is accepted, the photographer who submitted it is given the assignment of making the pictures. When the editors originate a feature lay-out idea, the picture-taking assignment may go to a staff photographer or to an outside cameraman.

The Sunday Department also buys individual photographs to illustrate articles both in the magazine and in such other Sunday sections as travel and entertainment. However, the illustration field is not much of a market. Pressed for time, the department selects most of its illustrations from the picture files maintained by established New York photo agencies. At last report, the basic payment rate for such illustrations was $12 per picture on publication. And if the picture is published again, the photographer gets an additional $12 for each re-use.

So much for the New York situation. In other cities most sizable newspapers have staff photographers but, as in New York, that doesn't eliminate all opportunity for the enterprising amateur. Then, too, there are papers which, instead of hiring staff photographers, arrange to give assignments to local commercial photographers if they will keep themselves available for calls. Anyone in a town whose paper does not have a staff photographer might consider suggesting such a project to the editor if he wants to devote most of his time to news photography.

A complete survey of the picture needs of every newspaper in this wide land is beyond the scope of this book. And to be really worthwhile it would require constant revision. However, we have made a sampling of some of the leading picture users in scattered geographic areas and have found they show a wide variation in requirements.

To present a fair idea of the range of the free-lance market, replies to queries mentioned earlier in this chapter are quoted. They will give you a first-hand report in each instance and help you decide where there is a possible market for your pictures.

If you are interested in any newspaper not among those we sampled, simply write that paper a letter asking specific questions. In most cases you will get an informative answer. If you don't, it is a fair assumption that the editor queried isn't interested in contributed photos.

Here are some of the replies:

William J. Barney, editor, Sunday Pictorial, Buffalo (N.Y.) *Courier-Express,* writes: "The *Courier-Express* Sunday Pictorial roto magazine gets all of its national and international material from the photo syndicate services to which it subscribes. In the local area, it buys an occasional photo story at $5 per photo (8 by 10 size preferred) but not more than $50 for the set. It buys no single shots, unless they are very out of the ordinary. Color photos, with a local or New York State significance, are bought at $25 for use of the transparency only. Nothing smaller than 2¼ by 2¼ is usable, 4 by 5 preferred. Vertical composition, of course."

The reason for that last phrase is simple. Though the *Courier-Express* is full size, the roto magazine is tabloid size. That means any pictures desired for full-page use must be verticals. And it is safe to assume that any color transparency worth purchasing would also be worth full-page display, very likely as the cover picture.

Sunday editor Bill Hosokawa of the Denver *Post* says: "Our photographic needs are fairly restricted in both quantity and subject matter. Our magazine is edited from a strongly regional angle, and so the pictures are selected from the same viewpoint. For many years we have run what is called Your Page, in which amateur photographers are encouraged to submit their efforts. Most of this material runs to scenics and other outdoor subjects, and we have received enough of these contributions to make up a large number of other pages. For our spot stuff, we depend almost entirely on staff photographers. We prefer prints 8 by 10, although we accept them postcard size from amateurs. The amateurs compete for $200 in prizes twice a year. In addition we pay anywhere from $2.00 to $7.50 per print, depending on quality and the use to which we put it. At present our color requirements are very much limited. We are considering transparencies

4 by 5 or larger. In time we hope to be able to use a larger number of color spreads in the inside pages."

Carl Gartner, rotogravure editor of the Des Moines *Register and Tribune*, replies somewhat similarly: "We buy free-lance photographs occasionally if they are exceptional as to quality or interest, but we don't want just run-of-the-mill stuff. Size makes no difference; it's quality we are after. Furthermore, we are mostly interested in material with an Iowa angle. We buy very little outside material that does not have an Iowa angle. We pay a minimum of $5 for black-and-white pictures and pay $25 for one-time use of color transparencies. Color must be at least 4 by 5 inches and need not necessarily have an Iowa tie-up. All this is for our Sunday Picture Magazine. There is virtually no market on our daily side for pictures unless they are spot-news pictures from Iowa or near Iowa."

The Philadelphia *Inquirer* boasts one of the largest Sunday circulations in the United States. And features that help it achieve that high total include the sections of the paper produced by Sunday editor A. C. Luther.

Mr. Luther reported that he had not been getting many offerings from free-lance photographers. He didn't know whether this was because of lack of material that met Sunday *Inquirer* standards or because of lack of space in his sections for contributions. Many of the photos used by the Sunday *Inquirer* merely illustrate stories that are predominantly text. Thus Mr. Luther cannot be very encouraging to the free-lance, but on the other hand he doesn't wish to discourage contributors altogether. Like most editors, he is always hoping that the mail will bring something so good it must be used.

As to specific needs, the Sunday *Inquirer* doesn't want and cannot use single black-and-white photographs no matter how beautifully pictorial they may be. To be acceptable monotone photographs must be complete stories. That means the photographic sequence should carry the burden of the tale. The text is secondary. Of course a completely informative general caption is nevertheless essential. So are cut-lines for the individual shots.

For color transparencies the rule is not so rigid. Both single shots and complete picture stories are considered. The caption requirements are the same. The preferred size for color submissions is the 4 by 5 transparency. The *Inquirer* will consider other size color photos but bars 35-millimeter and smaller shots.

Subject matter need not be restricted regionally to Philadelphia, its suburbs, the state of Pennsylvania, or even the nation. In fact the Sunday *Inquirer* is far from parochial. If a picture story otherwise meets requirements, there is no place in the world that is off its beat.

The reply from the San Francisco *Chronicle* offers very little hope for the free-lance amateur or professional cameraman. John T. Wallace, manager of that newspaper's Special Services, writes: "Generally speaking, the *Chronicle* does not encourage voluntary contributions from photographers outside this newspaper's circulation area. About the only exception to this policy is in the case of spot-news local pictures. Occasionally we purchase newsworthy shots from free-lances—provided, of course, that a *Chronicle* photographer or the AP is not on the scene—but that rarely happens more than once or twice a month. Our standard minimum reimbursement is $5; higher amounts depend on news value and exclusivity."

The *State Journal* of Lansing, Michigan, on the other hand, is quite encouraging. Managing editor K. R. West reports: "We are in the market for pictures only on a local scale except in exceptional instances when we have bought a few to illustrate Sunday features by writers in other parts of the country or the world. On every occasion that I can recall we have made such picture purchases from the writers themselves, either taken by them or acquired from their own sources for resale.

"We use a large volume of local pictures, mainly produced by our own photo staff, but we buy outstanding material from amateurs or professionals when we are not otherwise covered on the news events pictures. We are not equipped to use color pictures at any time. Size of prints is not too important as long as they are clear, contrasty photos which can be enlarged if necessary. Our minimum payment for usable prints is $3, with higher prices paid in some instances based on timeliness, quality, etc., of the picture and, in some cases, the trouble or expense involved in taking it."

Moving a little farther northwest, we reach the Minneapolis Sunday *Tribune*. Its rotogravure editor, Charles McFadden, says: "Although our Picture roto magazine is primarily interested in the Upper Midwest (Minnesota, North and South Dakota, and western Wisconsin), we definitely encourage voluntary contributions from photographers *anywhere*. Our requirement, however, is that features be outstanding and have universal appeal. We are interested in any features that we can duplicate. We prefer 8 by 10 prints. We pay a minimum of $5 per photo. We are also interested in color photos of outstanding subjects. They should be at least 2¼ by 2¼ in size and preferably larger."

The next two replies are put in sequence deliberately, because they are in striking contrast in the matter of encouraging and discouraging free-lance contributions.

On the encouraging side, we first quote Chester Gibbons, feature editor of the Seattle (Washington) *Times:* "The delay in answering your inquiry as to our photographic needs was deliberate . . . for I was in the process of attempting to raise our sights on payments to free-lances, both photographers and writers. I wanted to be able to give you an up-to-date scale. I am sorry to say, however, that my efforts produced but mediocre success, although I was given authority for more liberal 'bonus' payments where deserved.

"Our minimum payment remains $5 a print, except for cover shots, which may bring $15 to $25. Since we seldom buy a single picture for rotogravure, our payments are based on our judgment of the value of the lay-out as a whole, with the $5-per-print minimum as a yardstick.

"In the Magazine Section, where we use one or two pictures to illustrate a story, we may pay $10 a print on occasion; or, if the art is supplied by the author, we lump it in payment for the article.

"On the City side, we pay a minimum of $10 for spot-news shots, with bonuses for exceptional stuff. (There are a couple of ambulance-chasers who make a pretty good thing of it. They have car radios tuned to police calls.)

"As to our Rotogravure needs: we specialize in Pacific Northwest subjects. That is the big field for the free-lance photographer and writer. On general-interest stuff, national and international, we are more than amply supplied by the regular services to which we subscribe and it would be an unusual subject indeed that would lead us to buy a free-lance's layout that had no local angle.

"We prefer, of course, 8 by 10 glossy prints, but smaller sizes are acceptable. We usually call for the negatives of those pictures we select for publication. Not interested in color at present."

Now let's turn to Hal Fry, assistant Sunday editor of the Akron (Ohio) *Beacon-Journal,* for a discouraging statement. He says, "In the simplest language possible, the *Beacon-Journal* has no policy in regard to free-lance photographic contributions.

"Under normal circumstances we do not encourage submission of general free-lance shots, because we usually find that in the local field the proportion of those submitted that are usable is very small. The combination of irritation among those who have submitted them and the choice between facing the load of send-back work for rejects or facing the ire of those who send and find we have a 'no return' policy makes the going rough.

"So far as 'foreign' stuff is concerned, I think I'm safe in saying we go on the assumption that neither we nor any newspaper whose circulation is in the main limited to a given market area can sanely afford to bid competitively for material of top general interest. We depend on the syndicates.

"Recently we have—somewhat to our sorrow—invited submission of shots by amateurs for use in the new *B-J* Rotopix. The proposition on them is $5 per shot if used and a credit line. And no return of copy. We require 'statement of authorship' or whatever you want to call it, and written release of right to publish. In this category, of course, our interest is primarily in amateur coverage of local subjects—although we would, if we saw any, be glad to run outstanding stuff of anywhere done by people in our circulation district. Otherwise, on spot-news shots, etc., we look and bargain as the situation arises."

The Milwaukee (Wisconsin) *Journal* is somewhat more encouraging. Roto editor Robert Gilka advises: "Our stand on buying outside photographs is this: we maintain a large photographic staff and expect to fill most of our needs through this staff. However, we do buy some photographs, mostly singles of strikingly good quality and subject, short picture series of feature type, and color transparencies. Black-and-white prints should be 8 by 10. Caption material must, of course, be complete. There is no limit to the area from which such photographs may be accepted, although we concentrate on Wisconsin and Wisconsin subjects. The market here for color is limited, but we purchase some, no smaller than 2¼ by 2¼ inches, preferably 4 by 5. Rates for color run up to $75 a page (tabloid size). For black and white, rates average about $5 a print."

In replying for the *Christian Science Monitor,* Phil German, photo manager, wrote: "I have talked with the two editors who are most interested in encouraging readers to send photos. Mr. Herbert E. Thorson, our Family Feature editor, has given me a memo, I quote: 'The Family Feature Page of the *Monitor* encourages readers to submit photographs; both amateur and professional types of pictures are sought. Human interest, scenic, and unusual and odd are the main classifications. Average price is $3. Can't use color shots. Send prints to Herbert E. Thorson, Editor, Family Features Page, *Christian Science Monitor,* One Norway Street, Boston 15, Massachusetts.'

"Also a memo from Leavitt Morris, our Travel Page editor, says: the Travel Page encourages readers to submit vacation and scenic interest (with life) photographs: at least 2¼ by 3¼, black and white, tourist spots, and off-the-beaten-path resorts and areas. $3 average payment. Send to Leavitt Morris.

"In addition to photos received from our own correspondents, photos are also received with articles. As you know from your own long experience in the photo business, our needs are a little different and in some cases require a little extra research to secure the proper photos for our general news requirements. Also we receive the various syndicate services. As you know, the picture agencies furnish a large number of the request photos; also the agencies send from time to time selections on approval from which we can select for our files for future use; in this way we are able to build up a rather comprehensive file which saves time and is most helpful. We pay usual newspaper reproduction rates."

If you have the sort of subjects the *Monitor* uses, we can see nothing to bar either an amateur or professional with a fairly good negative file from submitting prints to Mr. German. He will reply promptly, returning unwanted photographs and paying for those retained for the files.

From across the border in Canada, James T. Annan, rotogravure editor of the Toronto *Star Weekly*, tells us: "We like photographers to submit 8 by 10 inch glossy prints. Negatives never should be submitted since if they ever are lost there is no way they can be replaced. We are also interested in color transparencies, but the transparencies should be no smaller than 4 by 5 inches in size and preferably larger. With regard to black-and-white subject matter, we are interested in high-quality single shots as well as sets of pictures. The subject matter should not be too industrial. Our *Star Weekly* circulates from coast to coast in Canada and as a result pictures must be of general interest. We pay $6 for each black-and-white photograph accepted for our use. We pay promptly on acceptance and unused pictures are returned immediately. We are happy to give a credit line to photographers whose pictures we use. We would be most happy to have photos submitted on approval. Return postage need not be submitted."

A possible, though perhaps infrequent, market is the *Deseret News* of Salt Lake City, Utah. According to managing editor Theron Liddle: "The *Deseret News* purchases occasional spot-news pictures from the Utah-Idaho-Wyoming-Nevada-Colorado area. Our Magazine Section also offers a market for good picture features with accompanying text on a strictly free-lance basis. The price of pictures varies from $2 to $5 depending on the subject matter and the quality."

A better-paying customer is the newspaper with one of the largest circulations in the United States, the Chicago *Tribune*. We confined our query to rotogravure picture needs, not those of the daily editions. From Leon Harpole, rotogravure editor, comes a specific outline of what he wants and how such pictures should be submitted. He writes: "The *Tribune* rotogravure section welcomes mailings of black-and-white photographs from any part of the world. Our preference is for human interest, action, and (in limited number) spectacular scenic shots, particularly with one or more human figures. In addition our roto section carries weekly a full or fractional page intended particularly for the work of amateurs. Requirements are substantially the same.

"Technically: Unmounted prints are wanted, 5 by 7 or larger, glossy preferred. Name and address should be on the back of each picture. Mailings should be addressed to Roto Editor, Chicago *Tribune,* Tribune Square, Chicago. Prints reproduced are not returned. Return of unaccepted prints cannot be guaranteed. Minimum rate in all cases: $7.50 per picture.

"Our needs for color are almost entirely supplied by our own color studio or other established channels, and only a very limited amount of color can be purchased from other sources. Minimum requirement as to size, 2¼ by 2¼. Payment is by agreement with the photographer in each individual case; we have no established rate for color."

We have already outlined the attitude of the Scripps-Howard chain regarding spot-news pictures. Here John Patterson, roto editor of the Pittsburgh *Press* of that chain, tells what he wants: "We definitely are in the market for contributions from free-lance photographers. But picture stories of local interest (involving persons and events in and around Pittsburgh) are more likely to be accepted. This is because we use a large amount of local material and are well covered nationally and internationally by our Metro Group and Acme services. We prefer 8 by 10 glossy prints and good contrast.

"Of the 52 covers we use in a year, about 48 involve local subjects. And these, with possibly one or two exceptions, are taken by our man, Stewart Love. His transparencies are all 4 by 5, though we have used 2¼ by 2¼. We shy away from 35-millimeter stuff.

"Minimum price per individual print is $5. And we pay a minimum of $25 for a picture story. Color payments are $25 to $50."

James M. Sheen, feature editor of *Grit,* Williamsport, Pennsylvania, is discouraging concerning that weekly's opportunities for free-lances: "Because of our connections with AP and Wide World, *Grit* purchases very few news pictures from individual photographers. However, we do buy a considerable number of photos to illustrate feature stories, usually from the writers who submit the stories. Our payment per picture is $3."

As you will notice from most of the replies, local picture coverage is emphasized in the Sunday sections as well as in the daily issues. The Providence (Rhode Island) *Journal* and the *Evening Bulletin* follow that trend. Sunday editor Garret D. Byrnes advises: "Our roto section, The Rhode Islander, regularly carries a page of photographs contributed by readers. The pictures are limited to the Rhode Island scene and we pay a flat rate of $5 for each one used. On several occasions amateur or professional free-lance photographers have contributed Rhode Island picture stories, or individual prints submitted have picture stories that could be developed. I think it would be fair to say that our going rate is $5 a print, higher prices being paid for exceptional photographs or for magazine cover shots. Being a state magazine, The Rhode Islander buys only pictures or picture stories with Rhode Island angles. We use no color shots editorially."

The Washington (D.C.) *Star* broadens its field a bit. Feature editor Philip H. Love explains: "The *Star* Pictorial Magazine is mostly interested in local picture features—or, at any rate, features with a strong local angle—but we do publish both articles and photos on interesting events, places, and personalities in other parts of the world. For black-and-white photos, we pay from $3 to $5 a print in some cases; in others, up to $15 a page, $25 for a double truck. We rarely use inside color editorially, but always have a color cover. Our top for 4 by 5 transparencies is $35 on a loan basis."

George Minot, managing editor of the Boston *Herald*, is another who holds out little hope for the free-lance: "We have such a large photographic staff of our own that we buy very few free-lance photographs. The exceptions, of course, are spot-news pictures, such as accidents and fires, where an outside photographer happens to be on the spot and gets a picture which it is impossible for our own photographers to get. Also we buy quite a few aerial photos for our roto and Sunday sections of new highways being constructed or a program of new bridges or housing developments and the like, which we can probably buy cheaper than sending up a plane of our own."

We wind up with a happier report from Julius Klyman, editor of Pictures, the Sunday rotogravure section of the St. Louis *Post-Dispatch.* He says:

"1. We encourage voluntary contributions from photographers anywhere.

"2. We are interested in almost anything good, but not manufactured. To be more precise, we are interested in news, features of all kinds, ranging from social, political, and economic problems to light, gay features. But the quality must be high. As to size of prints, we have no particular size we insist on.

"3. We are of course interested in the St. Louis area, but we are interested in anything any place in the world that is informative or entertaining.

"4. The above goes for both black and white and color.

"5. We prefer our color to be at least 2¼ by 2¼, although on occasions we have reproduced smaller color films. We also on occasion use 35-millimeter.

"6. Our price depends upon the value of the particular photographs submitted.

"7. We insist on complete information with submission of photographs."

To sum up, the sampling shows that by and large the newspapers are receptive to amateur and other free-lance contributions. But it also shows that just ordinary run-of-the-mill pictures won't go far in the roto and Sunday magazine field. Only the photographer with something original to contribute will be the one who makes picture sales.

The Market in the Magazines

ANYONE WHO CAN PRODUCE picture stories that crack the rotogravure and magazine sections of the Sunday newspapers is ready to try his hand on the weekly and monthly magazines. But before going into that field, spend some time taking stock. Think about the publications you aim at; think, too, about your own capabilities. And, as has been urged before in this book, consider carefully your chances of making a go of free-lancing as either a part-time or full-time career.

In periodicals, as in all other fields of photo journalism, the lot of the free-lance, man or woman, is precarious. We admire the courage of the photographer independent enough to strike out on his own; but that doesn't carry with it any admiration for his business judgment. Of course the rewards in money and fame for the photographer who clicks with the national magazines can be great. But the odds against reaching such eminence are unbelievably high.

Most of the successful free-lance photographers, in the exact sense of the words, aren't free-lances at all. Practically all first-flight, recognized photographers have fixed retainers or other guarantee arrangements that assure them a steady income year in and year out.

That brings us back to our original advice. Making and selling photographs for publication can be lots of fun. But usually it is fun only when free-lancing is a sideline, a hobby, or an avocation, not the sole or even principal source of income.

So take it easy. Don't even consider devoting all your time to magazine photography until you have become established as a fairly regular, though still a volunteer, contributor. When the magazines which have accepted your picture stories begin to give you assignments will be time enough to consider making photography your life's work.

To reach that goal is not easy. It may be a long, uphill struggle. It all depends upon how much originality in picture composition you have. Unless your work is distinctive and stands out above the general mass of shutter-bug production, stick to playing, not working, at photography.

The fellow who is so good that he can write his own ticket on retainers and fees doesn't need this book. Our efforts are directed toward helping the beginner and the occasional contributor—the amateur and the professional whose major occupation is commercial, photo finishing, or studio photography. For the amateur we are trying to provide guides toward gaining a little cash and a great deal more satisfaction and pleasure from his hobby. For the professional we hope this book will show the way to additional profits from the opportunities inherent in his present business. But for both amateur and professional, we repeat that contributing to newspapers and magazines should start as a sideline occupation—and should remain just that.

As to the possibilities of the magazines as picture markets, obviously only the high spots can be touched on in a book like this. So let us concentrate on some of those which offer the widest opportunities and pay the best prices. They should show the general pattern of the whole field and indicate procedures that will save time and money for both contributor and editor.

Unlike the newspapers and syndicates, the magazines, with the exception of *Newsweek, Time,* and *Life,* usually do not buy spot-news photographs directly from the men who make them. Of course at some time or other, practically every magazine prints photographs that are basically news pictures. But if you will check the magazines you read, paying particular attention to the credit lines for the photographs published, even a cursory glance will show you that in both the special picture sections and in illustrated articles, most of the photos have come from the large agencies. Those from AP, except in *Newsweek, Time,* and *Life,* will carry Wide World credit; Acme and International pictures will be so identified; and there will be a sprinkling of credits for the smaller agencies and for government-controlled outfits like Sovfoto. For the most part the editors of general periodicals have neither the time nor the facilities to run down photographs to the originating cameramen.

The news weeklies, *Newsweek* and *Time,* also rely on the major picture agencies to provide them with the bulk of their photographs. However, *Newsweek,* through its New York offices and its bureaus in Washington, Detroit, Chicago, and Los Angeles, will buy occasional pictures from experienced photographers. It is interested both in news shots and in feature picture stories to illustrate the departments into which the magazine is divided. In considering pictures for acceptance, *Newsweek* prefers they be exclusive to the magazine. Because it is interested only in the current news, news pictures must be delivered to it with the same speed as to a daily paper; both news and feature pictures must be accompanied by complete data from which the editors can write full captions.

Although *Life* has an exceedingly large staff of photographers assigned all over the world, it is receptive toward the free-lance contributor. It welcomes from voluntary contributors spot-news pictures that are exceptional pictorially, otherwise outstanding, and preferably exclusive.

Most of *Life*'s pictures, of course, come from its own sources or from the major agencies. Also because it is a member of the Associated Press, many of the pictures its own photographers make appear in the newspapers about as quickly as they do in *Life.* Nevertheless, even though a story has been well covered by the major agencies, an exclusive and striking shot has a good chance of acceptance. There is no limit, that we know of, on subject matter. Such pictures can be of fires, wrecks, war scenes, and other highly dramatic action. And sometimes news value can be very slight if the composition results in a highly dramatic photograph.

It may pay you to remember *Life* if you find yourself at a good story with plenty of competition from staff photographers of the newspapers and the press associations. If both your pictures and the story are good enough, fast submission to *Life,* instead of to the papers or the syndicates, may prove most profitable.

As for the details on how to contribute to *Life,* here is the magazine's own statement:

"The editors of *Life* advise that picture requirements cannot be summarized. There are no limits to their interest in whatever proves outstanding in photographic coverage. Prime requirements are for exclusive, dynamic photographs of spot-news events. Acceptance depends upon the importance of the news and photographic excellence. In the field of feature photography, emphasis is on the new, the different, and how well the pictures tell their story. Pictorial composition and all-around photographic excellence are essentials. In features originality, both as to the idea and execution, brings the best results. There is no limit on the photographer with creative imagination and the technical ability to create conceptions into outstanding photographs and/or picture stories.

"Because of page size and shape, contributors should realize that as a general thing verticals find readier acceptance than horizontal shots. That is especially true when full-page use is desired. However, don't limit yourself to verticals. Sometimes circumstances restrict the photographer to one position and one negative proportion. Whenever possible, move around for different camera angles and to produce negatives that can be enlarged to horizontal, vertical, and possibly square prints. Leave a little air in your negative to permit leeway in cropping. Some lay-out uses need that; others require close cropping; but the editors, not the photographer, decide. Captions, factual and complete, are musts. Though the deadline is Saturday, only the most important pictures will be considered then. The earlier your material arrives the better your chances.

"Payment starts at $100 per full page, for black and white, and $300 full page for color."

With the help of Ruth Lester, of *Life*'s Picture Bureau, we picked out three top examples of outside purchases. One, Marvin Goldman's Man in the Box series, which made the Speaking of Pictures section, is described in the chapter dealing with feature-picture production. The other two were both spot-news shots and were made half the world apart. Outstanding as the production of an amateur photographer is the general view of the bombing of Chungking, capital of free China, by the Japanese on June 28, 1940. It appeared as a two-page spread in *Life,* August 12, 1940.

Waldo Ruess, who made that picture, was and still is an amateur photographer. At the time of the Chungking bombing he was in China as an attaché of the American Embassy. When we wrote to him for information about his picture, he was at the airport at Keflavik, Iceland. But let's read his own account of the making of the bombing picture, called then "the best one taken up to that time."

Ruess writes: "I was stationed at Chungking from August 20, 1939, to November 3, 1942, with the American Embassy, which was then located on the south bank of the Yangtze, perhaps a quarter of a mile across the river from the city proper. It was 475 flagstone steps from the river (in low-water season at any rate) to my residence on the Ma Ngan Shan (Horse Saddle Mountain). I had an *f/2* Leica, a refugee's camera I had purchased in Shanghai in August, 1939, when en route from post at Tokyo to Chungking via Indochina. Previously I had used a No. 5 Leica bought in July, 1935, in Hankow and I used it until departure from Japan in 1939. I have taken several thousand pictures in fourteen of China's provinces—plus many in other countries (have visited in 66 countries, and am a member, Active Non-Resident, of the Explorers' Club). But, as you have been told, it is just a hobby with me, and I have not studied the hobby as even a good amateur should. My photography is perhaps more just reportorial in nature.

"After the first Japanese bombing near Hankow (Hanyang) I sent about two dozen pictures of the carnage and casualties by air to *Life,* thinking they might be interested. They didn't want any of them. This was in September, 1938.

"But I was in Chungking for virtually all of the 'good' (!?) bombings, with a grandstand view from across the river, and in comparatively little danger, as bombs were dropped on our side of the river only if they got stuck in the rack or through occasional mischievousness. Nevertheless, there were many that dropped as close as 100 or 150 yards, and I was about the only one of the Embassy who persistently refused to use the air-raid shelters. I am fatalistic, perhaps, about danger in such cases.

"After a couple of the 'good' bombings I thought I would send along some shots to *Life*. As I recollect, I said nothing whatever about any money for them. Shortly they wired back they were sending a check for $200 for one of them. About a week after that they cabled for me to 'get' the Generalissimo and the Madame [Chiang Kai-Shek] and also to collect album pictures of them. Perhaps they felt in my Embassy position I could more easily do this than even one of their own correspondents. Being in the Embassy I had to request permission for this from Ambassador Johnson—who vetoed it, saying I was there as an Embassy employee and not as a news photographer. Thus I lost a golden opportunity!

"The bombing picture was in an August issue of *Life* in 1940. On two subsequent occasions it was used, in smaller reproductions, $10 being sent me each time. Carl Mydans, who came there later, said my bombing picture was the best one he knew of having been taken anywhere in the world up to that time. Ralph Ingersoll of *PM* visited the Embassy in 1941 (when I was off in China's northwest) and told the Ambassador and others I should have been given $1,000 for the picture. Perhaps he has a peeve on *Life;* at all events *Life* claims I was given a good figure, the going rate at the time for such an occasion. Some well-known news cameramen came to Chungking during those war years, but somehow they seldom hit the place when there were 'good' bombings, and they couldn't hang around forever. If I had had a movie camera, color film, etc., I really could have made a killing. The picture in *Life* was taken from the balcony of my house on the top story; it was there, or from the Embassy, that I took most of the pictures, invariably with 135 mm. telephoto lens; as I recall the one in *Life* was taken at 100 with *f/6.3* opening and No. 2 yellow filter. I sent *Life* just a 9 by 56 cm print, and it was from this they made their two-page blow up for the August 1940 number.

"Afterward I sent some other bombing pictures to Black Star, who sold them to several English and European publications, giving me very small sums for my share. They advised me one was in the American 1942 edition of *Encyclopedia Britannica,* but I have never had the pleasure of seeing it. I think I received only $5, or possibly $10 or $12, for this. Now, they (*Life*) gave me, I believe, $10 additional for putting my bombing picture in the *Life* book.

"I now also have a Rolleiflex *f*/3.5, and a brand-new Leica, as my other was destroyed in a fire here. This summer I took some Kodachromes—ten or twelve rolls of thirty-six on a roll, in northern Norway, Finnish Lapland, Bavaria, Austria, and on the Dalmatian Coast. I do not do as much with pictures as I should; that is, I do not capitalize on my exceptional travel opportunities. Perhaps one day I will, *quien sabe?*"

There is no doubt that, as he himself says, Waldo Ruess, with so many opportunities for good pictures, is neglecting the marketing end. Few photographers get around the way he does. His assignments to China, Algiers, Tokyo, Moscow, and now Iceland gave him and are giving him unparalleled opportunity for picture making.

Of course, being so far from the market makes selling a problem. From his letter he seems not too happy with his returns through an agent as compared with those he received directly from *Life.* That is understandable, but he should realize that, at best, any agent remits only 50 percent of the sums received. That means the agent must sell a picture for $20 in order to give the photographer $10. When it comes to foreign sales, the return may be much smaller. When selling abroad, an American agent usually works through a foreign agent. Unless there is a special arrangement, the foreign agent remits to the American agent 50 percent of the foreign sale. Then the American agent splits that sum half and half with the contributor, so actually the man who makes the picture gets only 25 percent.

The other outstanding *Life* spot-news picture was much more recent than Ruess's It was made in New York City. *Life* gave it a full page on May 12, 1947. The caption used then is a complete description: "At the bottom of the Empire State Building the body of Evelyn McHale reposes calmly in grotesque bier, her falling body punched into the top of a car."

The photograph was taken by Robert C. Wiles of Eden, Maryland, who here tells how he got it: "The picture used by *Life* was one of a series of eight shots taken in a matter of a few seconds, before the cops arrived and took things over. I was attending the N.Y. Institute of Photography at the time, the location of which is just across the street. As the girl completely mashed the car top in, it wasn't necessary to get very high to get the right angle. However, I did get up on the bumper and hood for some shots.

"All told, I received $252 for the shots. *Cavalcade Magazine* in Paris, France, used one at the time of the incident. Later they were used by *U.S. Camera, U.S. Camera Annual, Readers' Scope,* and *Pageant.* The *Saturday Evening Post* bought one, as did *Real Story Magazine.*

"Am still in photography and have had many still shots used locally. I do all kinds of stuff from portraits to news. I like anything connected with photography.

"The camera used for the shots in question was a Retina 35-millimeter, exposures from 1/50 second *f/8* to 1/50 *f/16,* all negatives were good."

Now let us focus on a publication far from the spot-news field but one of the best of all periodical markets. The *National Geographic Magazine* is perhaps the most consistent patron of the traveling photographer. And it encourages free-lance contributions—so much so, that it has compiled a mimeographed sheet outlining requirements. Because in many ways the *National Geographic* is a wide-open market, and because its suggestions can be applied so generally, we are reprinting those instructions almost in full:

"In diffusing and humanizing geography the National Geographic Society requires for publication monochrome and natural-color photographs showing artistically and naturally the physical characteristics of every country and the manners, customs, activities, and costumes of every people.

"A most important requisite of the pictures used to illustrate the *National Geographic Magazine* is pictorial effectiveness obtained through careful attention in treatment of subject to composition and arrangement. Such photographs of the physical features of a locality including aerial views, typical dress, customs, festivals, occupations, industries, and amusements of the people become attractive and informative illustrations. Art and architecture of unusual or characteristic design, important public institutions and public works, scenes of historical significance, natural history and phenomena and always the 'strange and curious' provide subjects which help to present humanized geography.

"Whenever possible photographs should include people, preferably in action. Purely pictorial landscapes and other general views are usually improved by the inclusion of people, or in some cases animals, in the composition, if only to provide a scale. Readers are usually most interested in scenes showing how other people work and play—the folkways of our world. 'Types,' either unusual or attractive, always provide good subjects. Even a dull subject is enlivened by the introduction of 'human interest.'

"The size of the original negatives is unimportant so long as a sharp, clear print without grain is obtainable from it. In general a glossy print or enlargement about 6½ by 8 inches, showing full gradation of tones, is found most suitable for reproduction. Negatives are not required, although in some cases it may be desirable for the Society to borrow original negatives to make satisfactory prints in its own laboratories. Borrowed negatives receive the best possible care while in the Society's possession and are returned promptly by registered or insured mail or, if the bulk warrants, by insured railway express.

"Every issue of the *National Geographic Magazine* contains fifty-six or more pages of color illustrations.

"The same rules for subject and composition apply to both natural-color and monochrome photographs. In natural-color photography, however, it is essential to strive for true, clear, and harmonious color. Flat lighting, to avoid strong shadow contrast, will be found most satisfactory as a rule. Obviously, because of the vastly greater expense in natural-color reproduction, subjects which will appear as well in black and white should be reserved for that medium. There are several continuous tone natural-color films now available, of which Kodachrome, Ektachrome, and

Ansco color are the best known. Both the miniature (35-millimeter) and larger sizes of these films are satisfactory for reproduction. However, motion-picture frames are not suitable.

"Because *National Geographic* color illustrations are presented in series on multiples of eight pages, photographers are urged to submit a generous collection of pictures on a single subject so that a varied selection may be made. Color transparencies are usually purchased in groups of eight pages and rarely individually. Whenever possible, the leading picture of a color series is a full page vertical composition. The photographer should keep this in mind and look for subjects which would compose vertically and adapt themselves to the lead position in the series.

"Generous rates are paid for photographs upon acceptance, but these prices vary widely due to the condition under which the pictures are made and acquired. The *National Geographic Magazine* pays a minimum of $500 for enough natural-color photographs to make an eight-page series. For unusual material a bonus may be added.

"Color transparencies should be submitted in a form convenient for viewing. We prefer to receive them numbered, with the identifying captions of the entire group listed separately . . .

"Full rights to black-and-white photographs are not essential except in special cases, and the photographer may use them elsewhere if he desires after *Geographic* publication. However, good practice dictates that the same photographs should not be offered immediately to another American illustrated magazine unless the subject has definite 'news' value. A condition of acceptance of color photographs, however, is that they be not published elsewhere for three months after their appearance in the *Geographic*. All material published in the *National Geographic Magazine* is protected by United States and international copyright for the benefit of both contributor and publisher.

"Full information must accompany each photograph. Usually from ten to fifty words are sufficient to give the exact location, names of mountains, buildings, statues, or other features and to point out things of particular interest in the picture. The year within which the photograph was made also should be stated . . ."

In forwarding that form, Kip Ross of the Illustrations Division of the National Geographic Society wrote:

". . . Note in particular that we are the only magazine of national circulation which *prefers* 35-millimeter for color. Actually, more than 90 percent of all the color we publish is from 35-millimeter originals. Our reasons for preferring this size are that the quality of 35-millimeter Kodachrome emulsion is excellent and consistent; the film capacity of the 35-millimeter camera is great and permits many exposures in order to get just the right shot; the greater depth of the shorter focal length lenses avoids the ugly out-of-focus backgrounds—which are especially unpleasant in color; and the portability and flexibility of the small camera. Add to this the important psychological effect upon the subjects in that the most unsophisticated peoples of the world who are frequently photographed by our men seem less camera-shy than they would be if facing a bigger camera.

"Another point is that the average non-professional photographer who often does a lot of traveling most frequently uses 35-millimeter. This enables us to make use of those 'off the trail' shots that the professional frequently does not get.

"Advance queries frequently save the photographer time and expense, for we might happen to have something on the same subject in hand at the moment and would not require anything more at that time. We also like to know that something on a certain subject is available, and the query gives us a record for our files for future use.

"It might be worth mentioning that while we usually pay no more than $50 each for color pictures, this is not as low in comparison to other publications as it sounds. We almost always make up color series in eight- or sixteen-page sets, which usually use from ten to twenty-four individual pictures, whereas other periodicals which may pay more for individual shots use less in the total. Our flat rate of $500 for eight pages or $1,000 for sixteen pages is based on the average of ten or twenty pictures in either case."

One thing Ross did not mention is quite an inducement to many contributing photographers. It is the *Geographic*'s policy to print the photographer's credit line under each and every reproduction. That is especially valuable for those who hope to get orders from publications and individuals for pictures from their files. The name under the picture is noticed, while a credit line in a box, hidden well inside the magazine, may be overlooked.

In this sampling of magazine requirements we are deliberately passing over magazines in special fields. Publications like *U.S. Camera, Popular Photography, Popular Science Monthly, Mechanix Illustrated,* and many others tell right in their names what they want pictorially. Similarly, there is no need to survey industrial and trade publications, because the photographs they want obviously will be those keyed with their subject matter. Not to be overlooked, however, is *U.S. Camera Annual.* Though few are aware of it, the *Annual* welcomes contributions from individual photographers. It isn't necessary to have had your photographs published locally or nationally or to have someone nominate your work. If you think you have something that will make the grade, simply send it along. The rules are simple:

Subject matter: No restrictions or preferences.
Quantity: Number of prints unlimited.
Size of prints: No larger than 11 by 14; 8 by 10 preferred, glossy and unmounted.
Photo Data: Wherever possible, photo data is desirable and should include camera, film, shutter speed, lens, aperture, lighting, date photo was made, title or subject, model release, and exact credit line required.
Return postage should be included, otherwise prints will not be returned.
Payment for use of prints is made upon publication in *U.S. Camera Annual.* Payment is in addition to a complimentary copy of the *Annual.*
Prints are for *U.S. Camera Annual* only and this includes use of prints in connection with promotion, publicity, and reviews of *U.S. Camera Annual.*
Prints not selected for *U.S. Camera Annual* may be considered for use in *U.S. Camera* magazine unless specifically restricted by the photographer.
Appearance of photographs in other publications does not preclude their use in *U.S. Camera Annual.*

Of course the *Annual* is a once-a-year proposition. But inclusion in it carries prestige. And because prior publication is no bar, it may mean another fee for a picture that has been previously sold, not just once, but many times.

Look magazine uses a great many photographs. Apparently that should make it a good market for the contributing photographer. Actually it isn't. Too much of its material is produced by staff photographers. And being a biweekly, with 26 instead of 52 issues a year like the weeklies, also cuts its picture consumption. Nevertheless, the free-lance has some chance, as picture editor Joseph J. Wurzel of *Look* makes clear in the following outline of his magazine's picture needs:

"Pictures of 'people' as distinct from 'things' are most likely to please *Look* magazine. Frankly, it is a hard-to-crash but, nevertheless, interesting market for the picture man who can come up with the unusual in subject, technique, or in treatment. Because it has a staff of ten top-notch cameramen, the free-lance has an added hurdle to overcome in finding a home for his submissions. But if you are lucky, the resulting distinction is worthwhile and the scale of payment is good.

"Pictures which fall into the 'human interest' classification, whether they feature dogs, cats, horses, etc., or humans themselves, rate high with *Look's* editorial board. Where they have sequence, the acceptance rate is likely to be higher still.

"In submitting his pictures the free-lance should never send negatives unless he is specifically requested to do so. Eight- by ten-inch enlargements are acceptable, where available; otherwise contact prints will do. They should, of course, be adequately identified and captioned so that your purpose in taking is not left to chance."

For the photographer with a bent for scenic and travel pictures, a good market is *Holiday.* Louis Mercier, its picture editor, points out that only a small fraction of the photographs used in its fifty picture pages each month come from volunteer contributors. But if you read his detailed instructions, you will find his magazine is always on the look-out for good photographers:

"*Holiday,* a Curtis publication, with as many as fifty pages open to color and black-and-white photographs, attracts a very large volume of unsolicited photo submissions by amateurs and professionals. These provide the editors with a small proportion of the photographs that appear in the magazine. The majority are procured by assignment.

"*Holiday* editors plan in detail the picture lay-outs accompanying the articles, before any pictures are procured at all. This means that space is alloted to the story on its importance; each 'spread' of two facing pages within that space is assigned a theme; and individual subjects within the theme, and supporting it, are assigned positions in the spread. The structure of a spread frequently undergoes changes on the lay-out tables, according to the caliber and composition of the pictures; but the number of spreads and their themes are revised downward or upward only in cases of unusual failure or extraordinary excellence of the coverage.

"While a subject is 'in work' from the time planning begins until pages go to engraving, the editors encourage submission of existing stock material on that subject. They do not release lists of subjects in work, but they will give a 'yes' or 'no' answer to queries regarding their interest in photographs of scenes or activities in a particular country, United States, state, or city.

"Picture sets that tell a complete story, preferably about a place or some aspect of life there, also are considered for outright purchase.

"Moreover, the picture editor will view samples of a photographer's work with an eye to putting him on the assignment list if his style fits in with *Holiday*'s requirements.

"Pictures submitted—whether as samples for consideration in connection with a particular subject, or to fulfill an assignment—must conform to certain standards. For color, original transparencies are required, preferably in sizes 2¼ by 2¼ or larger, although 35-millimeter of truly exceptional quality will be considered. Each transparency should have a concise, but complete, caption affixed to the bottom of a transparency cover. This caption should include the photographer's name. Black and white (8 by 10 or 11 by 14) should have captions affixed to the back of each print or along the bottom.

"It is not easy to land on *Holiday*'s assignment list. But Herm

Nathan (who is now one of the staff photographers of Graphic House in New York) stopped at *Holiday's* Philadelphia office on his way east from the University of Ohio to start his career after completing his studies and so impressed the Picture Editor and the Art Editor that he was encouraged to shoot some pictures on a subject then in work. These were used in the famous New York issue of *Holiday*, which sold out a press run of more than a million copies and was reprinted in book form.

"One of several transparencies submitted by Walt Duke to be considered for use with a story on Montana was used as a *Holiday* cover.

"Some of Roger Coster's stock photos of Paris scenes were bought up when his agent submitted them to *Holiday* a few years ago, and Coster now puts in almost all his time filling *Holiday* assignments.

"*Holiday* is interested in young photographers and in new ideas in photography; but interested photographers are advised to submit well-selected and well-captioned samples, stock photos, or picture sets, and to watch *Holiday's* pages for signs of what the editors want. They do not as a rule want personality stories, industrial, or quick trips over great distances. The magazine's stock in trade is the story about the life and character of a particular place."

Although words outbalance pictures by a wide margin, another Curtis publication, the *Saturday Evening Post,* uses a great many photographs. Some of the photographs are simply illustrations; quite often pictures predominate in a feature lay-out, with text relegated to general caption and cut-lines. Douglas Borgstedt, Photography Editor of the *SEP,* outlines his magazine's requirements:

"The *Post* is basically a text magazine, although this does not mean we minimize the importance of pictures. But, broadly speaking, it does mean that we obtain our text matter first, and then procure the necessary pictures to illustrate it. It is the exception, rather than the rule, when we obtain pictures first, and then base text matter on them.

"We do not employ a staff of salaried photographers, but call upon the services of free-lance photographers through the country and the world according to our needs. However, we do give anywhere from two-thirds to three-quarters of our assignments to a group of about a dozen photographers, who more or less act as an informal staff group. We keep these men fairly busy, and pretty much have first call upon their services. In return, about half of this group do not work for magazines that are directly competitive with the *Post.*

"The remaining percentage of our assignments go to free-lance photographers based on the particular needs of the assignments, plus such other factors as geographical location, or perhaps the peculiar requirements of the assignment, or the special talent required for an individual job.

"In a few instances we have agreements with photographers that we will provide them with a certain amount of work during the year. For example, this is true in Washington, D. C., where we feel that we must always have a photographer available at all times.

"In addition to photographs that illustrate articles we run occasional picture stories. These are generally in color, consisting of a lay-out from six to ten pictures, with sufficient information and story material for a short text of 500 to 1000 words. Generally this text is written by a staff writer here in the office, based on the information which is supplied with the pictures. The best way to submit picture-story ideas is in the form of an outline of two or three hundred words, containing sufficient information so that we can evaluate it. Or, the complete picture story with the pictures already taken can be submitted.

"Most of the unsolicited pictures which we buy are in the form of these picture stories. But it is the exception, rather than the rule, when a photographer goes ahead and undertakes the expense and trouble of shooting the whole picture story without querying us first with an outline as to whether we like the subject or not.

"We have a fairly regular schedule of prices, but since no two jobs are exactly the same, I think it would be unwise to quote them here. Our prices compare favorably with those of other popular magazines, although we pay by the assignment, rather than by a page rate or a day rate."

If you are a steady reader of the *SEP*, you will note that Mr. Borgstedt did not mention another current opportunity for free-lance picture contributors. As this is written, the *Post*, every few weeks or so, prints a single picture with short text in a two-column box titled I Am Proud of This Picture. The going rate is $100. A small-type note in each box tells what is wanted and how prints should be submitted.

Like the other two members of the Curtis family of publications, the *Ladies' Home Journal* is a limited but good-paying market for free-lance photographers. Picture Editor John Morris tells what they want:

"It's difficult to outline our requirements because they are exceedingly flexible. Almost all our photographs are now done on assignment, and we are not considered a good picture market from the standpoint of quantity purchased. On the other hand we do pay well for pictures when we buy them. We welcome the submission of pictures and picture ideas. They can be sent either to the picture editor or, if the photographer prefers, to the departmental editor concerned—fashion pictures to the fashion editor, architectural pictures to the architectural editor, etc. We make no technical stipulations.

"At the moment probably the greatest opportunity for the free-lance photographer is that of making the *Journal* cover. We have also bought, from time to time, a good many black-and-white pictures of children to illustrate Dr. Bundesen's articles on child care, have occasionally bought scenes for decorative purposes, etc. We are open to suggestions for our major departments, such as 'How America Lives,' but prefer in this case to see an outline or preliminary pictures so as to waste the time of neither the photographer nor subject."

With his reply Mr. Morris enclosed a form letter which the *Journal* has been sending out. Dated May 30, 1951, it reads:

AN OPEN LETTER TO PHOTOGRAPHERS

In August the *Journal* will publish the fifteenth and last of the "Undiscovered American Beauty" covers. They have been selected from more than three thousand candidates submitted by photographers throughout the country during the past twenty-three months. We are grateful for this response and only regret that so few could be chosen. We could claim, with some justification, I think, to have the most beautiful "rejects" in the business.

The *Journal* cover will continue to be open to ideas and photographs submitted by professional photographers. We shall follow, as in the past, a policy of variety. We shall continue to watch for pretty faces, "undiscovered" or not. We shall look for beauty in fashion, in flowers, and in the expressions of children. We are open to suggestions which break with previous cover tradition. For example, we feel that the possibilities of romanticism in cover photography have scarcely been explored. Direct realism also has its place. Above all we must look for covers which have broad appeal to women.

For the "Undiscovered" series it was possible to set a standard price. In the future prices will be subject to negotiation.

John Morris
Picture Editor

Some may dispute mentioning the next two weekly publications here rather than in the chapter discussing newspaper markets. While both are circulated as part of Sunday newspapers across the country, from an editorial view and from that of the contributing photographer, they should be considered national magazines. We refer to *Parade* and *This Week.* Of the two, *Parade* is the better prospect for the free-lance contributor. Jess Gorkin, its editor, outlines its photographic needs.

"*Parade* likes *good* pictures of many sorts," writes Gorkin, "but especially pictures of people doing everyday things, and animals.

"We like picture stories that have a direct interest for every family, picture stories about interesting personalities, out-of-door sequences, stories about children. We also like an occasional good sports set.

"One of the best pictures we ever used was one that photographer Arthur Shay happened to run across in Pittsburgh. Shay saw an old piano standing on the sidewalk. It had been left there because movers couldn't fit it through a doorway, and Shay spent two days simply snapping 'candid' shots showing what happened to that fine old piano—and how various people stopped to play it, how the police came, how kids gradually began to tear it apart, how a man with a sledge hammer finally smashed it up, in great glee, and left it to be hauled away.

"The important thing about the story is that Shay not only got a fine set of photographs, but he did a splendid reporting job as well. He not only took pictures of the people who stopped to play—but he found out who they were and what they played!

"This is an ideal example of good picture material for *Parade*."

This anecdote points up sharply a point we have made repeatedly: a good news or feature photographer must always be a doubly good reporter. *Parade* is full of picture stories. To get in they must be good reporting jobs—with camera first, but with words almost equally important. Although Mr. Gorkin doesn't say so directly, his emphasis on Shay's reporting should tell you that accurate, factual, and complete captions covering the entire story must accompany picture sequences submitted to *Parade*.

If you can get hold of one of the Sunday papers that includes *Parade*, study a copy. Doing so will give you a far better idea than any words what kind of material clicks with it. Editorial standards are very high, but once they are met, rates are good. And the door is wide open for contributors.

This Week is a far more difficult market to enter. In a memorandum detailing what it wants occurs the phrase "articles that lend themselves to dramatic pictorial treatment." That indicates a feeling for pictures but points up the fact that *This Week*'s emphasis is primarily on text, with photographs for the most part serving merely as illustrations. *This Week*, however, uses color transparencies on its cover, paying excellent prices for such photographs. And there is an occasional opportunity for the contributing photographer in double-page feature-picture spreads. Such lay-outs are found most of the time in the edition of *This Week* that is part of the New York *Herald Tribune*. For actually *This Week* is almost two magazines, with a great many features, such as picture spreads, fashion, and purely *Herald Tribune* material, appearing only in the edition circulated with that New York newspaper.

We have left to the last one of the widest, but far from the easiest, markets. Crowell-Collier issues three national magazines, one weekly and two monthlies, that use a great many photographs. Both in color and black and white, *Collier's, Woman's Home Companion,* and the *American Magazine* do a bang-up photographic job. Most of the material comes from regulars who get assignments. But not all of it.

James A. Quigney is *Collier's* photographic editor. But because at one time or another he has had his finger on the picture pulse of all three magazines, we asked him to outline the requirements of all of them. If you are interested in hard nuts to crack, read what he has to say. He writes:

"All three of the Crowell-Collier publications have used full-color photographs for covers. At the moment the *American Magazine* is using nonphotographic art for its covers. How soon, if at all, it will return to the use of color transparencies, in whole or in part, I can't say. While *Collier's* for the most part selects photographic art for its covers, paintings, and even sculpture, and other types of art are used on occasion.

"The only definite limitation we have on color transparencies is size. We don't want anything smaller than 2¼ by 2¼. That applies to all three magazines and for the inside illustrations as well as cover art.

"Any photographer who wants to break in with a cover shot for our publication should carefully study several issues. That's the best way to get an idea of what is wanted. A variety of shapes may be used inside the book, but cover transparencies must approximate the proportions of the page. That means vertical compositions are desired, as all the magazines are longer than they are wide. Even though square film sizes are used, the pictorial composition can leave air on both sides of the transparency so the finished picture is vertical.

"Cover contributions should be addressed to the Picture Editor for *Collier's* and to the Art Directors for the other two magazines. Though no decision can be made until the finished transparencies are delivered, a query with a written outline or a sketch of the proposed shot is usually a good beginning. Then the editors can advise whether the idea has possibilities and, if it has, make suggestions that will increase the chance of acceptance.

"For *Collier's* only," Quigney continues, "we are looking for feature-picture stories in full color. The transparencies should carry the tale. Text should be kept to a minimum, though without eliminating essential information. The main caption must be complete as well as brief. The individual transparencies should carry cut-lines describing those shots. The cut-lines or individual captions must include full names of all persons pictured, their occupation, title, rank, or other identification, and the date the exposure was made.

"The number of pictures used in sets like that varies widely, depending upon the space allotted and final printed size of the pictures used. Contributors aren't advised to waste film, but on the other hand it will pay them to make enough exposures to provide a liberal quantity for editorial selection. Photographers may submit advance outlines of feature-picture possibilities or completed picture-story packages.

"*Collier's* also likes to know about capable cameramen who can cover specific assignments in either black and white or full color. Anyone interested should write to the Picture Editor. He should briefly list photographic qualifications and experience, equipment, availability for assignments, including transportation available and how far he is willing to travel, and the like. If on the basis of the letter, the Picture Editor is interested, he will reply asking for samples and additional data for inclusion in his file of available photographers. Samples should not be included with the first letter.

"Along the same line, we also like to know about photographers anywhere who maintain files, both in black and white and color, of scenic views, animal shots, architectural, travel, and aerial views. Though the main interest for stock is on the part of *Collier's*, occasionally there are such calls from the *Woman's Home Companion.* When black-and-white pictures are wanted the preference is for 8 by 10 prints. Negatives should not be sent along unless specifically requested.

"Turning to the particular needs of the other Crowell-Collier publications, the Picture Companion section of the *Woman's Home Companion* offers opportunity to contributing photographers. Picture stories of a strictly service nature to women, such as cooking, cosmetics, and beauty culture, child care, home maintenance, decoration, fashions, and the like are wanted. As an example, I recall that one set submitted by a photographer showed how a little girl properly cares for her fingernails. Issues of the *Companion* carry as many as sixteen pages in the section. There are several different lay-outs. The aim is to provide enough variety in topics and photographs to achieve the desired editorial and pictorial balance.

"For this section, queries in outline form should be submitted for approval before picture shooting starts. If the idea is approved, the photographer will be told to go ahead. At the same time suggestions and modifications will be offered to meet editorial desires. All communications about such feature pictures should be addressed to the Art Director of the *Woman's Home Companion.*

"The *Companion* is also interested in powerful picture articles covering serious problems of interest to women. Here the idea should be submitted to the Article Editor, who will discuss it with the photographer in case the magazine is interested.

"The *American Magazine*'s best opportunity for the contributing photographer is the Interesting People department. There is no preference as to method here. Written outlines or complete packages of pictures and text will receive prompt consideration. Only one picture is needed as a rule, with about 500 words of text, to make a package. Either should be addressed to the Editor of Interesting People.

"Sometimes color is used, but for the original submissions one 8 by 10 black-and-white glossy is sufficient. If more black and whites are needed or a color transparency is wanted, it will be ordered from the submitting photographer. Stories to be accepted must have national not just local interest.

"And as a last word, I can't mention specific rates of payment because there is such wide variation depending upon the material and the use to which it is put. But I can say that all our publications pay very well and the rates compare very favorably with those of other magazines in our fields."

The "Little" Markets

ALMOST EVERY PHOTOGRAPH that is clear, well composed, and tells a story can be sold to someone, somewhere. The difficulty is finding that someone and somewhere. Much too often concentration on top markets results in overlooking profits that could be gleaned from lesser purchasers.

There is no question that the quickest and probably the largest cash returns come from hitting the jackpot with an outstanding spot-news picture. But that's a less than once-in-a-thousand-lifetimes chance. Feature series and cover-picture sales to leading magazines are also very profitable. Yet they also are understandingly infrequent. By all means go after them when you have something they might use. But you can try for spot-news and cover sales and seek out the smaller markets too.

For example, money can be made by submitting prints to publications and advertisers with highly specialized needs. Don't let the fact that they buy few pictures scare you off. If you have something right on the target for them, your chances of making a quick sale are good. Sometimes they will buy pictures that can be sold nowhere else but are very welcome in that specific market. And often you can sell them photographs that have already had a good run in the picture syndicates, newspapers, and national magazines.

If you have any doubts about this advice on selling the same picture more than once, just reflect for a moment. The fact that a photograph can be sold over and over again is what keeps the picture syndicates in business. Of course, they get calls from markets the lone free-lance never hears about. But they also have expenses and overhead that he doesn't have. Anyone with a fair knowledge of possible outlets, some envelopes and postage stamps, plus a willingness to do a little intensive selling by mail can get the ultimate dollar from every single picture or photo sequence he produces.

A friend of ours proved that recently. He is Con Gebbie, specializing in photographs for the public-relations department of the Shell Oil Company. That spot gives him the advantage of acquaintance with markets and a location in New York near some of the big users of photographs. The possible disadvantage, which didn't stop him, is the fact that most editors are used to his sending them handouts, *i.e.*, free photographs that publicize his firm. The sequence we refer to had nothing to do with his company, and in every instance he made cash sales. We'll let him tell you how he did it:

"I am firmly convinced that any competent free-lance photographer can more than double his usual income—and do it without shooting extra picture stories, too. It's all a matter of making a few extra prints, spending a little more on postage, and knowing the market.

"Take Elmer Lens, for example: he gets a bright idea for a syndicate picture spread, rushes into it with his usual enthusiasm, comes up with good pictures, and makes the sale. Good, that was an easy $100. Now what? And here's where Elmer misses the boat.

"Fired by the success of the last idea he starts immediately on another, hoping for another quick sale. He may, or may not, make it—but in the meantime he has a sure-fire thing right in his hands, a story that brought him $100, a story that has appeal because it sold, a story he has already done. Why doesn't he sell it again, and again, and again? But Elmer probably won't even try, and for two reasons: (1) he thinks the story is dead because it got wide circulation from the syndicate, and (2) the other possible markets are small and probably won't pay much, anyway.

"Elmer is wrong on both counts. His story is far from dead, and the other markets do pay well when lumped together. As a cold matter of fact, they actually will return him more net profit than his first big sale, for the simple reason that Elmer must write off expenses against that original $100. He has no expenses for the sales to follow, other than the making of prints and the buying of stamps.

"Let me give you an example from my own experience. I shot a ten-picture story on a small-town editor in Hawarden, Iowa, with *This Week* magazine in mind. The story turned out well and I sold it for $150. The magazine has one of the largest circulations in the world, and by all counts the story was dead after *This Week* used it.

"But I didn't think so. I made three more sets of the same story, changed the captions a bit, and began hitting the markets the average free-lance usually passes up because 'they don't pay enough.'

"Well, the Sioux City (Iowa) *Journal* bought the story for $28. The daily *Argus-Leader* of Sioux Falls, S.D., bought it for $25. *Publishers' Auxiliary* used it and sent a check; *American Press* made a nice spread; *Grit* used it. It sold to two house magazines of companies in Iowa ($30 and $35); it was bought by a printing-equipment outfit ($15). In all the story sold twelve different times after the first sale. It brought in an extra $250 which, compared with the original sale of $150, is quite satisfactory. And that same story will sell for another three or four years. Each sale is small, of course, but is a net return for the simple business of addressing a new label, making a few prints, and shooting the pix out, a matter of a few minutes each time."

That Gebbie is not overestimating possibilities, every picture-syndicate sales manager knows. In fact I recall one classic example of three separate syndicates handling the same set of pictures over the course of a few years. That's as far as I followed it. The pictures may be still selling, though I haven't noticed any of them recently.

The photographs to which I refer were made on an expedition to South America. As it happened, the photographs turned out to be much better than the expedition. The first rights were sold to Times Wide World Photos, on a basis of cash for use in the subscription service and royalty on sales to non-subscribing publications. Wide World borrowed the negatives and divided the best shots into three or four or perhaps more sets that were widely distributed and published in the United States and abroad. About six months later the negatives were returned to the owners. They promptly interested another syndicate, which gave them a second whirl, hitting publications that for one reason or another Wide World didn't reach. Then about two years later we began to notice the pictures—slightly different shots but the same expedition—appearing with a third syndicate credit line. As Gebbie so clearly indicates, there is no reason why that cannot be done more often and by free-lances as well as organized picture-selling firms.

In seeking those extra sales, don't overlook the little items in your pictures. A strand of rope dangling from a ship or dropped from a helicopter during a rescue mission may make your photograph readily salable to a rope manufacturer. We mentioned earlier Frank Seed's shots of the helicopter rescue at Niagara Falls; the rope manufacturer sought him out to get those pictures. Automobiles, tractors, trucks, and many other objects with identifiable trade marks that show up in your pictures may bring extra sales. But it would hardly be bright to try to sell a picture of a wreck to the maker of the cars involved. And don't be blatant about showing names and trade marks. You should be thinking of news first and making pictures that newspapers can and will use. Don't emphasize commercial aspects to the extent that you spoil the news value of your photos.

Now, for details on potential non-news markets: it would take at least a separate volume to list all the possibilities in the field of specialized interests. There are trade and class journals, house organs, window-display services, state and locality publications. Often purely scenic photographs that other buyers wouldn't take as a gift can be sold to state publications or to a state, city, or county publicity bureau. The price range may be low, as little as $2 to $5 for black and whites. But that will at least pay film and print costs.

In the class and trade field you will find a great many publications. They cover almost every field you can think of. There are farm publications, house and garden magazines, sports journals—some covering the field in general and others covering a particular sport like golf, tennis, baseball, and so on—aviation magazines, juveniles, religious journals, and magazines devoted to food, transportation, textiles, etcetera.

Just as for newspapers and general magazines, your attempts to make a sale to these should be preceded by a query. But getting names and addresses of those in the field you wish to broach may be a problem. Those of you who have ready access to public libraries will have an easier time of it. There you may find the *Directory of Newspapers and Periodicals* published by N. W. Ayer, the *Writer's Guide,* and the *Universal Photo Almanac,* to mention a few of the guidebooks. If you have no luck at the public library, try your local newspaper. It may have one or more of these books in its reference library.

Whether or not you have access to a directory, you should check first-hand the publications to which you wish to submit photographs. You can buy most magazines of general circulation at the nearest newsstand. Some of the larger trade and class journals are available there too. For the others and for house organs, check local retailers and wholesalers of nationally advertised products. A good many of them will subscribe to the trade papers in their fields. And if house organs are issued by the manufacturers of the articles they sell, they are very likely to have copies.

For example, practically every automobile dealer has the house organs, at least, of the makers of the cars he sells. Very likely he will have one or more of the automotive trade papers. Department stores subscribe to many magazines covering the various types of merchandise they handle. There are publications for operators of hotels, restaurants, motor courts, trailer camps, and many other business lines, including, of course, photography. Tracking down and looking over all these will be hard work. But it will be worth it in time and money saved by *not* sending pictures to non-existent or the wrong markets.

You will discover that some of the house organs are ambitious publications. Those like *Ford Times, GM Folks, General Electric News,* and *Chevrolet News* often buy general material at prices that compare favorably with rates paid by the national magazines. Many more, while buying little or nothing from volunteer contributors, do make photographic assignments. One that we know of is *Us* issued by the United States Rubber Company. Getting assignments from this company magazine is as difficult as getting them from most other types of publications. But the rewards are as high, too.

There are other house organs that are good markets for interesting photographs showing out-of-the-ordinary uses of the products made by their companies. Some of the trade and class journals also use pictures along those lines—good photographs of products in use. According to the latest directory, more than five thousand house organs are published in the United States. Not all of them—probably much less than half of them—are potential customers for the free-lance photographer. But enough of them are to make efforts at crashing that market fairly profitable.

In seeking contact with those house organs that use general pictorial material, procedures should be the same as in finding out what magazines of general circulation want. Letters of inquiry will get you the information. For those that use no general photos, we have found the best bet is to wait until you happen to make a picture in which the company's products appear. If it is easy to make an extra print, send one along, with a complete caption, of course, and a formal release (permission to print) from the individuals pictured. If that isn't convenient for one reason or another, write asking whether the firm is interested in pictures of their products and describing in detail what your picture shows. We have found that unless you have already had direct contact with someone else in the organization, it is best to write to the advertising department of the company, rather than to the editor of the house organ, when you wish to submit product pictures. You have a better chance of making a sale, because even though the house organ may not want your picture, the company may be able to use it in advertising, sales promotion, or just-for-the-record files. What department buys it should make no difference to you, just as long as they pay for it.

Even for spot-news pictures, such as fires, accidents, earthquakes, storms, and other natural phenomena, the newspapers and syndicates are neither the only, nor necessarily the best-paying, outlets. Of course, it's wise first to get to the markets requiring utmost speed. But don't dawdle in trying also the insurance companies and the trade papers in the insurance field. Some companies specialize in certain forms of insurance such as fire, automobile, accident, and the like. Others cover the general field. Reference books and the advertisements of the big companies will tell you the range of their interest. Local insurance agents or brokers can give you all the dope you need about the companies they represent. Because window-display services often have insurance companies as clients, they also may be good customers for such pictures.

But you don't have to stop there. The principals in an auto accident, for instance, are also potential customers. Frank Seed of Niagara Falls says he never overlooks an opportunity to sell such pictures to one or the other participant in auto accidents. He usually tries to sell his pictures to the fellow who appears to be the injured party. For of course you can sell prints only to one side.

Except that it may mean your having to be a witness at a trial, following up an accident for sales does not require much extra work. Most of the information must be gathered for your news captions, so all you have to do is make an extra copy. For legal purposes, exact time and location, probably including the direction in which you pointed your camera to photograph the scene, may be necessary in helping the interested parties decide on liability.

Getting back to the insurance companies, they are interested in fire, accident, and calamity pictures for a variety of reasons. Some use them in house organs; others use them either in direct sales or fire-prevention advertising copy. When you offer pictures for such sales, make certain about the use to which they will be put. Normally, the rate for use in an advertisement is many times the amount paid for a single publication in a house organ.

Another well-paying market for photographs may be found among the printers of calendars. Calendar use is an advertising use, so releases from individuals pictured will be needed. It also means rates of payment should be high. Calendar printers also use many scenics without people.

Finding out who the printers are and what pictures they want is easy. Look around your own home town. Examine the wall calendars you find in homes, banks, railroad stations, stores, and shops. Somewhere, under the picture or elsewhere on the front, you will find the name and address of the printer who issued them. Check the local merchants who distribute calendars to learn the sources of those they give away. Then, as in other efforts to sell pictures, write a letter of inquiry. Ask not only whether photographs are wanted, but what type, size, and finish, and whether black and white or color is desired.

We come now to a field that is not one for the amateur, or, for that matter, for the professional who has other interests—advertising photography such as appears in the paid display ads in newspapers and magazines. While our main effort in this book is to lay a course for those seeking a market for spot-news and feature photographs, we feel our readers should have some knowledge of other photo markets. In advertising photography such knowledge can prove helpful even if for most readers it indicates only a field to avoid. It can also be of help to the adventurous, imaginative camera enthusiast who, despite the enormous obstacles, wishes to explore another facet of photography for pay and publication.

The obstacles in advertising photography are indeed many. When you try that game you are moving in very fast company. The rewards are high—very high, at times—but the competition is keen. And unlike the news field, display advertising offers practically no opportunity for a photographer to stumble upon a situation that will give him a chance to produce a salable picture.

In advertising the concept—the whole plan of an advertising campaign—is worked out long before there is a definite decision on the type of pictorial copy. In most news photography the lay-out is made to fit the pictures, but in advertising the pictures are made to fit the lay-out. Hence, art editors, when they assign photographers, know exactly or almost exactly what they want. They choose a photographer with whose work they are acquainted and on whom they can rely to produce what they want. In other words, they seek experience. And getting experience, always a hard job for a newcomer, is perhaps even harder in advertising than in any other field.

James E. Clark, Jr., art director of Cecil & Presbrey, a New York advertising agency, points out: "There has been very little need for us to go looking for photographers to hire. Occasionally, and I should add, very rarely, we have an advertising campaign for which we must make pictures in the field. If the job is important enough to rate the expense, or very technical, we assign an experienced advertising photographer from New York. If it is not so important or if the pictures desired are not so-called advertising art but more nearly news type, we seek out local men. Usually in such cases we go to the local newspapers for recommendations. If they have staff photographers, we try to use them. If they haven't, we hire a local man who contributes news pictures to them.

"That method has worked fairly well on two recent jobs," Clark adds. "Both were for the Texas Gas Transmission Corporation. One assignment was to show how employees of the firm moving into new communities blended with the older residents. Any local man well grounded in the fundamentals of news photography could make the pictures we wanted—individuals standing in line with other residents at the bank, post office, supermarket, at PTA meetings, and the like. But you would be surprised to learn how hard it is to find men with news sense, who will get away from stilted stiff groups with everybody looking at the camera and no signs of life or activity.

"The other assignment for Texas Gas was to show pipe-line construction. That I would consider a straight news job. And luckily we got a good news cameraman to make the pictures. We were very pleased with the results.

"But," Clark goes on, "these have been the only opportunities in this shop along these lines in years. And even then the news men were restricted to making photographs that would fit into exact shapes and sizes in our advertising lay-outs. We sent them rough outlines so they would know what they were shooting at."

Pointing out that the odds against the beginner might perhaps be shortened if he knows what's wanted, Clark continues: "Let's talk about the current trend in advertising photography. Right now, and this will surprise the fellows dependent upon flash bulbs and photofloods even on outdoor locations, the trend in advertising is to natural daylight. And I don't mean on location. I am referring to studio work. The old-fashioned studio with its wide areas of good clear north windows is back in style.

"Objects photographed with natural light look natural. They have none of the hard, brittle, unnatural look that is so common when high-powered floodlights and spots are used. And there is less strain upon the models. They can pose naturally without the intense heat that cannot be avoided with the use of artificial lighting powerful enough for photography. And may I digress here long enough to point out that in much advertising photography the right model is more important than the cameraman? The model must have the qualities sought for the advertisement. Then it takes a good cameraman to transfer them through the lens of his camera to film. If the qualities don't exist, the best cameraman in the world can't get them on film.

"Now, I will try to answer the questions most pertinent to the aspiring photographer who wants to know how to break into the advertising game. First I shall start out by being discouraging. It's a tough racket. While there are many doing very well, there are many more just getting by or slowly starving. Breaking in is very difficult. I can recall only one recent instance of a news photographer who came to New York and successfully crashed the gates of advertising work.

"He came here when advertising photography was mainly extremely stilted, brittle, and dead. He put his news background to use to infuse into his pictures a sense of naturalness and life that caught on. There is always room for the gifted individual who has something to contribute. But, too often, knocking at the gates for recognition can be a heart-breaking process.

"As a matter of fact," Clark goes on, "the photographer in the smaller places has a better chance to get advertising photo experience than the fellows in big cities like New York, Chicago, San Francisco, Los Angeles, and others. That is, if they are not too small to have an agency.

"In the big cities, with all the established photographers to choose from, art directors, naturally enough, are very reluctant to experiment with unknowns. That probably isn't true in smaller places. So local agencies must rely on local talent. If you feel you have a flair for advertising illustrative photography, stay home and practice with your local advertisers. When you have done enough to convince yourself that you can really make a contribution and have a good portfolio of pictures and the advertisements that used them to back you up, you are ready to break into wider markets."

Mr. Clark does point out, as we have earlier, that there is still some market among house organs for pictures of products in use. Payment isn't high; the usual range is from $5 to $12 per print, which is hardly enough to warrant seeking out such objects to shoot. But if you run into such pictures, they can prove a profitable sideline.

Here is one instance of how such a sideline deal worked out. In 1949 or '50, when the local power company in Tucson, Arizona, was building a new electric generating plant, it commissioned Western Ways to make a series of progress pictures of the construction job. Naturally, among those pictures were shots of one company's control panels, another's boilers, a third's generators, and so on. Those photographs were separated, captioned, and then mailed to the advertising departments of the respective companies. Checking names and addresses required a little research; there was a small expense for prints and postage, but it was all worth it. Most of the companies bought pictures at rates of payment for intended use. Some ordered new photographs at commercial rates to show their apparatus installed. Only a few returned the prints unused.

One important caution: If recognizable persons appear in your photographs, these photographs cannot be used for any commercial purpose—and that includes sales brochures and house organs as well as other advertising—without a release from each individual pictured. Individual releases are required also by most magazines for cover pictures and for some other illustrative uses. So, because releases are so important when you get away from straight news photography, we are printing a specimen form, with the suggestion that you consult a lawyer if you have any doubts about its conformance to the laws of your state.

CECIL & PRESBREY Inc.
ADVERTISING
247 Park Avenue, New York, 17, N.Y.

Date.............., 19

CECIL & PRESBREY, Inc., and

....

New York, N.Y.

Dear Sirs:—

For valuable consideration received by me from you, the receipt whereof is hereby acknowledged, I hereby certify that I am of full age and have every right to contract in my own name, and I hereby give and grant to Cecil & Presbrey, Inc., and

....

and to their customers, agents, licensees, successors and assigns, free and unlimited right and permission to use, publish and republish, for any and all trade purposes or commercial advertising, photographic prints of me or any reproductions thereof or parts thereof, photographic or otherwise, with such additions, alterations or changes therein as you in your discretion may make, and to use, publish and republish the same, either separately or together with my name or a fictitious name, or the name of another person and/or any advertising statements or testimonials made by me or purporting to have been made by me which you may, in your discretion, prepare for use in connections therewith.

WITNESS my signature the day above written.

Name ....

Address ....

Witness ....

Address of Witness ....

The undersigned, being the parent or guardian of the above named, for a consideration received, hereby consents to the above release and signature.

Name ....

Address ....

Witness ....

Address ....

From advertising to publicity photography seems a natural step. In the sense that both are commissioned by a person with something to sell, be it an idea or merchandise, they are alike. In photographic techniques there is quite a difference, however.

As we have seen, advertising photography is a highly specialized form of picture taking. Publicity photos, however, are not very different from spot-news or feature pictures; indeed the whole aim is to give them the appearance of news though they serve some promotional purpose.

So the best course for the cameraman to follow in making publicity photographs is to stick to the rules for making spot-news and feature pictures. In those, the photographer wants to produce something editors will buy, and he can do that best by getting a story on film as graphically and truthfully as his mind, camera, and film permit. In publicity shots, the cameraman also wants to produce pictures that editors will "buy"—in the sense that they will print the photos. But his story now must succeed in getting his client's message across to the reader. In other words, the photographer has the double chore of making his pictures newsworthy, of stressing his client's angle, or playing down things that might hurt his publicity. It's not easy, but it is being done all the time.

Right here we should point out that it would be a waste of time and materials to work up publicity picture stories on speculation. Practically all publicity photos intended as hand-outs are made on assignment, with the press agent originating the idea. So if you want to make publicity shots, get an assignment first. You go about securing one just the way you seek out any commission. Once you have the assignment, you follow through as you would on a news-picture job. Study your story and figure out the best approach. A shooting script will help as much here as it does in any other type of picture story. If you can't get a script, try to get a rather good outline of what is wanted in the way of pictures and what is back of the publicity story. Then you can work out the details, making up your own script. It will pay to know budget limitations, how many negatives are wanted, and whether the story is intended for picture services, newspapers, magazines, or some one particular spot.

Though the primary responsibility for the truthfulness of publicity material—and that includes photographs and captions—rests with the press agent and his client, the photographer should always be watchful of his own reputation. Don't be a party to misrepresentation. It is all right, and in fact quite proper, to help your client put his best foot forward in the pictures you make. In your shots, floors in a factory should look clean; people should be observing safety regulations and other laws. It would be bad, to say the least, to show workmen smoking under a "No Smoking" sign. But don't falsify the setting.

Sometimes hired models are necessary in a publicity story. Equally often they are out of place. The experienced photographer can help the story by indicating where and when they should be used. In making fashion pictures models are obviously essential. And fashions frequently help other publicity. For years pictures of pretty girls in bathing or sun suits and riding bicycles have been used to popularize bicycles, not the fashions.

Photographers and press agents have long found that giving away straight news pictures of important happenings has great publicity value. In 1933, when Mayor Anton Cermak of Chicago was fatally shot in the attempt on the life of the then President-elect, Franklin D. Roosevelt, Steve Hannagan's Miami Beach publicity photographers covered the news story and Hannagan made their pictures available to newspapers and syndicates without any thought of publicity tie-in. The good will of the press was worth much more than any publicity mention.

More recently, within a 48-hour period two Air France planes crashed into the Persian Gulf at almost the same spot. On both occasions Tommy Walters, who had been sent to Saudi Arabia to make publicity photographs for the American-Arabian Oil Company, flew to the crash scene with U.S. Air Force rescue missions. He made pictures; his film was processed hurriedly on Bahrein Island and air-expressed via TWA to his company headquarters in New York. There the pictures were turned over to the major press associations for news distribution without any request for credit to the company. Performing a public service like that is smart publicity for both the photographer and his employer.

Hundreds of top news pictures have been publicity-inspired and have put over a publicity message as well as making news. This isn't the place to cite all the instances, but outstanding was circus press agent Frank Braden's exploit in getting a midget to sit on the lap of J. P. Morgan at a Congressional hearing back in 1933. Publicity pictures also made the United States Siamese-twin-conscious, according to Terry Turner, who managed and promoted all of them except P. T. Barnum's real Siamese pair, Eng and Chang.

Turner, who is now exploitation chief for RKO Pictures, hired photographers to take pictures showing how the twins did every-day things despite their handicap of permanent union. The two sets of girls, Daisy and Violet Hilton, from England, and Mary and Margaret Gibbs, from Holyoke, Massachusetts, were of course better camera subjects than the men twins. However, Turner had pictures taken of them all, sleeping back to back, eating meals at home and in restaurants (where waiters brought two chairs and then confusedly discovered the twins could use but one), playing musical instruments, applying for marriage licenses (the Hiltons had a public wedding in the Cotton Bowl), riding in automobiles and streetcars, and so on. And the newspapers gladly printed these hand-out shots. Such pictures, says Turner, did more to make the public pay to see the twins than pages of advertising and news copy.

Even though the photographer may not want to make publicity-picture making a full-time commercial occupation, he can take a fling at it. Often employees of big companies have a chance to contribute pictures made at and away from the plant to house organs and other company publications. The rewards may vary. Sometimes they'll be just credit lines, sometimes regular payments, sometimes prizes in contests. Many companies encourage camera clubs both for bettering employee relations and as a source of pictures. The U.S. Rubber Company not only favored such clubs at its plants, but even provided rooms and fully equipped laboratories so the club members could do their own processing.

Though we do not commonly think of orchestras and bands as business in the ordinary sense, they are business organizations nevertheless. And they offer much better opportunities to the amateur photographer than less glamorous enterprises. Many musicians have found opportunities to make pictures that they could sell for publication. And a number of orchestras have found it less disturbing, both to the conductor and to his musicians, to have publicity pictures made by one of their own members rather than by outside photographers.

For more years than we can remember, Arturo Toscanini's musicians have been "sneaking" candid shots of him at rehearsal. It seems to be no secret that the maestro was aware of their activity. Some of the musician-photographers have sold their pictures directly to publications. Others have given them to the National Broadcasting Company for publicity purposes. Of course, Toscanini's much publicized aversion to flash bulbs and to posing for professional photographers didn't lessen the value of the candids made not only by his musicians but also by his son, Walter Toscanini.

In order to glean a few pointers to pass along to you on how to make pictures of a conductor and fellow musicians from a bench in the orchestra, we spoke to Carlton Cooley. He is first viola in the NBC orchestra and a prolific maker of Toscanini candids. Fifty to seventy-five shots is his estimate of the pictures he has caught of the conductor. Oddly enough, Cooley is a simon-pure amateur. He has never sold a picture and has no desire to. But he does get a kick out of seeing his photographs published and has turned over many negatives to the NBC publicity department. His pictures of Toscanini have appeared in *Newsweek, Time,* and other publications.

Because he must shoot quickly and has time to aim only when the score allows a few bars' rest for the violas, Cooley does all his focusing, setting of camera stops, and the like, before Toscanini calls the orchestra to attention. And he takes all his photos at rehearsals, never at performances where his actions might distract the audience.

On days on which he plans to take pictures, Cooley goes to the studio an hour before rehearsals start. Using anybody as a stand-in, he focuses from his seat, about seven feet from the conductor's podium, to get the exact setting that will catch Toscanini in sharp focus. Then he sets his shutter speed and fixes the lens opening. When he began his picture taking, Cooley took exposure-meter readings. Now he knows the studio lights so well that it is no longer necessary. During rehearsals his camera lies in his lap, all ready to be picked up, aimed, shutter released, and film and tension wound up for another shot whenever a good Toscanini pose coincides with a rest for the violas.

Cooley graduated from box cameras to a No. 12 Argus 35-millimeter less than ten years ago. He soon moved up to a Contax. His camera is equipped with a Zeis Sonar *f/1.5* lens. Normally he shoots wide open at 1/25th of a second. Once in a great while he tries 1/10th of a second. But with this speed, movement has spoiled too large a percentage of the exposures.

Those who want to make copies but haven't room for large equipment will be interested in Cooley's discovery that a 35-millimeter outfit set up as a copying camera produces negatives that easily enlarge to 5 by 7 and 8 by 10. He has found it especially valuable in copying scores of musical compositions. The results are as good as and perhaps better than other methods, and certainly much faster.

There are always markets for the fellow with a novel idea. Phil Mikoda, a top color man on the Ansco staff, is interesting police departments in the use of color photography. It helps in crime detection. Black and white may not show it, but it's easy to tell a bloodstain from a grease spot on a color transparency or print. If your town law-enforcement agency doesn't have a photographer and if you are good at color, right there may be an opportunity for you.

In concluding this discussion of miscellaneous markets for news and feature pictures, we should look at television. Because of the nature of the medium, most telecasters prefer movie strips. However, many stations, including some of the big ones in New York, use some still pictures on news broadcasts and for other purposes.

The field is too new for us to lay down any broad rules on picture taking for TV. At best television can be but a limited market for the amateur who has only a still camera. There may, however, be a bit more opportunity for the fellow with a small movie outfit. For both stills and movie strips, the market will depend on a station's own facilities for getting picture coverage. If you are interested in TV picture making, your best bet is to check the situation with your nearest television station.

Tips from the Professionals

ALL CAMERAMEN HAVE some little short cuts or special ways of doing work in the effort to produce better pictures. Or they may have worked out ways of smoothing the path in taking pictures. That is especially true of the professional photographers. Some of them are a bit secretive about how they do things, but most are quite willing to pass along helpful ideas and methods. In this chapter we reveal some of their secrets.

For instance, Frank Seed of Niagara Falls, should know a great deal about honeymooners. He does. And honeymooners are important in his business. Making spot-news stills and movies is for him a sideline, though a very profitable one. A more dependable and routine source of income is taking group shots of tourists at the Falls.

Honeymooners are the best purchasers of such photographs. So Seed concentrates on them, making certain that they are right up front where they can be seen in the picture. Naturally he cannot ask questions to find out who, among any group, are the brides and grooms. Early in the game Seed found a quick and an infallible way of spotting honeymoon couples. If the male half of the pair is wearing new shoes, they are newly-weds, says Seed.

A professional photographer who has traveled widely abroad warns that overseas it is a good idea to safeguard cameras and other gear from light-fingered gentry. At home, he says, he has no compunctions about letting his camera dangle loosely at the end of a shoulder strap. But when abroad he keeps a firm hand on his gear. He himself lost nothing on his latest trip, but he did see a quick theft that made him increase his own precautions.

Ahead of him one day another traveling cameraman strolled down a street with a Rollei swinging from a shoulder strap. In a flash a native youth sped down the sidewalk, flipped the strap off the owner's shoulder, and was a block away before the camera was missed.

Now we are not suggesting that cameras are never stolen right here at home. They are and much too often. Cameras are valuable; there is a ready market for them, and they seem to be easily "fenced" loot.

So newspaper staff photographers and other professionals warn you not to leave cameras lying in plain view in parked cars. That goes also for closed cars with windows all rolled up and all the doors locked. Windows can be and have been broken and door locks can be picked or forced. This doesn't mean leaving your camera at home when you are driving. It should be with you. But it does mean that if you must leave it in the car, lock it up out of sight if you can. The glove compartment is ideal for small outfits. Bigger cameras and the accompanying gear should go into the trunk. If this is impossible, at least put your equipment on the floor, not the seat, and cover it with newspapers, an old coat, or anything else that will hide it from the sharp eyes of a sneak thief.

The next tip isn't strictly for the news photographer, but it may prove helpful to those whose whole picture effort isn't slanted toward news. Every photographer has had trouble with dry-lipped subjects. Grown-ups can be told to wet their lips before the shutter is snapped. You can't use that method with the very young. Robin Garland, now manager of the Photo Journalism Department of Graflex, worked out a neat solution of that problem when he spent most of his time making children's portraits. He stuffed his pockets with lollipops wrapped in Cellophane, five different colors and flavors. The sight of them made the children's mouths water and produced automatic smacking of lips. When that wasn't quite enough, a preliminary taste of a favorite flavor solved the dry-lip problem.

Another professional, Murray Becker, chief photographer of the Associated Press, advises amateurs and other free-lances not to be scared away by the presence of large contingents of staff photographers at major sports events. This goes especially for big outdoor affairs like baseball and football games. Most of the professionals assigned to major events find their movements fairly restricted. Usually they must stay in photographic stands built on top of stadiums or hung from the fronts of upper stands. Big berthas with extra long lenses overcome some of the resultant handicaps of fixed position, but not all.

The free-lance in the stand often has a better vantage point for some of the best action in the game. If he is on his toes he can find a market for his shots either with the daily papers or the magazines, which in this instance should include Sunday sections of the newspapers. The free-lance also has an ideal spot from which to make human-interest pictures of his neighbors as they go through facial and other contortions to root for their teams.

The games sometimes result in spot news too. Becker reminds us that on July 4, 1950, when a spent bullet fired from a neighboring roof killed a fan at a baseball game at the New York Polo Grounds, it was the camera-carrying spectators nearby who got the pictures of the dying man slumped in his seat. By the time the professionals could hurry over from the photographic stands across the stadium, the body had been removed.

Each time there is an eclipse of the sun or the moon, everybody with a camera tries for a picture. At least so it seems from the deluge of pictures that have flowed in to us after every major eclipse. Photographing an eclipse poses two problems. One is the weather, and nothing can be done about that. If the clouds hide the sun or the moon, the photographer has to give up.

But if the weather is with you, then the following paragraphs should help you plan for pictures of the next eclipse. Frank Jones, staff photographer of the *Twin City Sentinel,* Winston-Salem, North Carolina, chose the photo he made of an eclipse of the moon as his best picture of the year 1950. In a recent edition of his paper, he wrote a first-hand account of how he planned and made that shot. Here is his account, quoted in part:

"To photograph the progressive phases of the eclipse," wrote Jones, "required more than three hours. The equipment put to use was the standard 4 by 5 news-type camera fitted with a war surplus 20-inch aerial telephoto lens.

"The camera was placed on a tripod on top of the Journal-Sentinel Building after first checking with the local weather station to determine what the sky would be like. Since the sky was crystal clear the night of Monday, September 26, it was what I would call perfect picture-taking weather.

"Seven test exposures on three types of film were first made and developed in order to determine the correct exposure. An exposure meter was of course out of the question. The test exposures were made on fine-grain, infra-red, and high-speed films. The latter gave me what I needed.

"Getting the moon in sharp focus was a problem, for it was constantly on the move and did not appear bright on the focusing glass of the camera. A magnifying lens was used to check focus. The exposure was computed to be at an *f* stop of 8 exposing each phase of the moon for 1/30th of a second.

"Computing the path of the moon as it glided across the film was a problem and frankly I guessed at it. This as you can see was a good guess.

"Exposures were made at half-hour intervals in order to show phases of the eclipse. On the print it is possible to see the outlines of the craters but reproduction of course destroys much of the detail.

"The white cloud appearance has nothing to do with the eclipse. It is the reflected glow from the city light on the haze above the city. It certainly adds to the pictorialization and somehow adds depth to the whole picture.

"Development of the negative was for four minutes, and the print was made on regular glossy paper for news reproduction.

"There are two other aspects of the creation of this picture which I believe might prove interesting. First, there could not be any retakes. The first and only picture had to be it. One mistake and the entire idea would have to be tabled. There were no mistakes, I am happy to say, because the picture was carefully planned and executed. Between the first and second exposures (camera was constantly being checked before and after each picture, for gremlins somehow creep in) moisture condensed on the lens and it was necessary to cover the lens except during the short exposures.

"There being seven separate exposures on the same film the question of why is there no negative fog might come up. The duration of each exposure was so very short that the possibility of outside light creeping in was nil. Also the exposures were not nearly long enough to record any stars.

"All this seems to stress the fact that really good pictures (and I consider this one good) are seldom made on the spur of the moment. My best pictures are always planned just as a writer of a news story plans his lead and the angle the story is to take.

"I am also very proud of this picture for one other reason and this is: no other newspaper in the state had a picture of this heavenly phenomenon and for once I couldn't say: 'Just one more shot, please.'"

Besides the technical data, which should be mighty helpful if you want to go after eclipse pictures, we recommend careful rereading of the next-to-the-last paragraph in Jones's account. His remarks about planning should be remembered and heeded in every photographic chore you face.

All the professionals aren't newspaper staff photographers. Some, like Charles Phelps Cushing, run their own picture agencies. Cushing's staff is small. He and Mrs. Cushing do everything but the processing, which is farmed out.

Cushing has his office on 42nd Street in New York, a few flights up, overlooking Pershing Square and in front of Grand Central Terminal. His window commands a view of the continuous traffic on the cross streets and along the elevated highway that bridges 42nd Street and skirts around the Terminal to rejoin Park Avenue.

With all that traffic, minor mishaps are likely to be frequent. So Cushing is prepared to respond to the crash of metal and the squealing of brakes when accidents occur. He keeps his Graphic camera open on a desk near the window. Film is always in place; the lens aperture is set at *f/11;* the shutter is at 100; and the bellows is racked back to the infinity setting. All Cushing has to do when news breaks on the street below is cock the shutter of the camera and swing his outfit into place at the open window, ready to shoot any action.

Also helpful should be Cushing's account of why and how he made the two pictures that have sold best for him. One required careful preparation. The other was the direct result of his keeping his eyes open for picture possibilities on a motor trip through New England. Both prove it doesn't take the lucky chance of being at the scene of a spot-news happening to make your camera bring in cash returns.

First for the picture that required careful planning. Cushing knows that there is a steady demand for skyline shots of New York. He also knows that for best results a photo should be made when all the piers along the Hudson River are filled with ships. So instead of rushing across to the Jersey shore at the first opportunity, he waited until every slip was filled and the light and the weather were exactly right. That happened on September 11, 1939. Five big ocean liners were in port. Left to right, in his picture, he caught the *Roma, Queen Mary, Normandie, Île de France,* and *Champlain.* Though some of those vessels are no longer afloat, customers are still buying that shot.

Cushing got the picture from above the West Shore tracks of the New York Central System in Weehawken, New Jersey. It was made on 4 by 5 pan Eastman roll film in a Graphic camera, using a filter for clouds and setting the camera on a tripod for long exposure.

The other Cushing best-seller is a picture of a church at Litchfield, Connecticut. He made it simply because it seemed to him a typical New England church in a typical New England setting. It sells for the same reason.

The only caption he puts on it is the name of the church and the town. Long after he pictured the building, Cushing learned its history. It is the First Congregational Church built in 1829 on the site shown in the photo. In the late Victorian era it was moved away because the congregation decided to build a newer and more "modern" edifice. Years later the members of the congregation realized that the old building had historical value. So they razed the new structure and moved the old church back.

It was after the final move that Cushing, motoring through Litchfield, made the photograph.

Some of the tips in this chapter will direct you to other markets. And such sales are always welcome, for being able to sell the same photograph to more than a single prospect often means converting a losing assignment into a profitable one. The major syndicates as well as the smaller agencies have found that out. Sales to the high-paying big publications are the frosting on the cake; making overhead and enough more to provide a profit margin often comes from other sales. The steady stream of small buyers who purchase for a wide variety of needs from advertising and other publication uses down to collectors who want to paste prints in scrapbooks are very important.

That brings us to some more hints from Bob Garland. When he and Mrs. Garland were working up a children's portraiture business as a sideline to his magazine efforts, he found a simple way to get cash in advance for print orders. The unfinished prints were the bait he used. They were submitted with a printed form that read:

"THESE ARE UNFINISHED PROOFS"

> "Proofs are to show expression and clarity of the photographs. Final tone, range, depth, and quality of the finished portraits are not shown.
>
> "It is suggested that you mark instructions as to quantity, size or change on the back of these proofs and return them in the mailer. An addressed label is included for that purpose.
>
> "Should you wish to own the unfinished proofs, include payment for your order when returning the proofs and we will send all proofs back with the finished portraits prepaid. Otherwise finished portraits will be shipped C.O.D. plus nominal mailing charges."

Bob relates an experience in the news-picture field that might help anyone anxious to make air views without paying plane hire. It means watching and being ready to take advantage of opportunities.

The incident occurred years ago when Garland was just breaking into newspaper work, and before he became an accredited news photographer. Garland learned that for publicity purposes one of the big oil companies was giving sightseers free airplane rides from a Boston airport over the city and harbor. He also knew that one of the big ocean-racing yachts was due to arrive the same day. So Bob borrowed a camera, found out the yacht's arrival time, and went to the airport, waiting to get in line for the free ride until such time as would assure his being over the port of Boston as the yacht came sailing in.

Everything worked out as planned. He took an excellent picture of the yacht, escorted by a destroyer and other harbor craft, sailing into Boston. And it was a half-page smash on page one of a Boston roto the following Sunday. Bob has forgotten the amount of payment, but he never will forget the thrill of seeing that picture in print.

Later on when he was working in Philadelphia, he worked out another profitable picture operation. The suburb in which he and his wife lived was quite sport conscious, with local events every week-end. Depending upon the season, there were baseball, football, or basketball games.

The town had two newspapers, so Bob made deals with both of them to provide picture coverage and rush prints of the week-end sports events. Next he arranged to supply enlargements for display purposes to local storekeepers. Finally he went after sales to individuals—those in the pictures and others interested in the events. Producing prints for all those outlets often meant missing much sleep and working day and night every week-end. But often these week-end profits were much greater than the salary for a full week's work at his regular job in Philadelphia.

From another professional come the following hints—the results not only of his own experiences in covering news, but of watching amateurs miss the best shots at spot-news happenings. Too often, he says, amateurs are overcautious, spending much too much time focusing and making other adjustments of their equipment, when instead they should be snapping the shutter. He says that everyone who wants to cover news should practice handling his gear until every action becomes second nature and almost reflex action. Taking pictures should be like driving an automobile. Most of the things drivers do when they guide a car through traffic are semi-automatic responses to road conditions. If a driver had to give conscious thought to the location of brakes, gearshift levers, clutch, gas throttle, etcetera, the highways would be even more dangerous than they are.

Camera operation should be equally automatic. The mechanical acts—such as racking out the bellows, setting shutter openings and speeds, pulling out the slide—ought to require a minimum of conscious thought. The conscious emphasis should be on shooting fast, before prime action is over, quickly recognizing best positions for shots, and getting pictures that tell the story. Our professional says the main thing is to shoot, not to wait for the better opportunity that never comes.

He points out, too, that for action pictures that look like action, a little movement in the photograph helps create the illusion. That means using slower shutter; not so slow as to blur the entire negative, but not so fast as to stop action sharply. There has been a fetish about stopping action. Camera and lens manufacturers emphasize exposure speeds. They talk about stopping action. That's fine. Sometimes it's necessary, but too often it is overdone. We recall one very striking example of that in which we were personally involved.

Some fifteen or maybe more years ago, one of the British racing-car drivers was about to make speed trials on the hard-packed tidal sands of Daytona Beach, Florida. So we, for Times Wide World Photos, sent a photographer from Miami up to Daytona to cover the tests.

After the first day's trial run we got a wire telling us that the undeveloped negatives were coming air express. The wire also told us that our photographer had stopped action by shooting at top shutter speed in the bright Florida sunlight.

When his films were developed we found he was too right. He had stopped action all right. In fact he had stopped it so successfully that his pictures looked just like the shots of the car standing still before the speed trial started. With no background but the ocean, and that far enough away to be an out-of-focus blur, there was nothing in his photographs to give an impression of speed.

We immediately wired instructions to shoot slower, telling why. It took two days and the exchange of many telegrams to put the lesson across. We finally got the pictures we wanted. There was just enough blurring of the car to make it appear to be moving. That produced the illusion of speedy motion that provided photographs worth publication.

Though the professional friend whose advice we have been relaying has stressed the importance of shooting fast at the news scene, he also stresses taking the time, when it can be done without sacrificing other advantages, to make pictures that are different. Too often photos look as if the man behind the camera simply pointed and shot without thought. They lack imagination. As an example he points out that at fires cameramen have a wide-spread tendency to get back and shoot too many general views. On fire assignments some general views are certainly necessary, but they shouldn't be made to the exclusion of close-up dramatic action. Getting close to people doing things is standard advice that should be heeded.

Storms are a possible exception to that rule. Usually nobody but a photographer is foolhardy enough to be abroad when the weather gets very rough. The tip on storms is to shoot everything —but be careful about getting too close to anything that may come loose and fall on you. Pictures of swaying trees, poles, and structures made at the height of the storm are always newsworthy. So are pictures of fallen buildings, and the like, made after the biggest blows are spent. With luck you may get some real action during a storm, but you will need all your luck, not only for that, but to keep out of the way of flying debris and falling poles and trees.

A yarn told by James A. Quigney of *Collier's* describes an avoidable unhappy experience that probably happens to every photographer at least once. That's forgivable. Repetitions aren't.

A long time ago when Jim Quigney was handling photographs for *American Magazine,* he assigned ace portrait-photographer George Higgins to make portraits of Thomas A. Edison. Accordingly Higgins packed up his equipment and took a train to Menlo Park, West Orange, New Jersey.

That is a short ride from New York, so Higgins arrived early in the afternoon. When he met Edison, he didn't open his camera. Instead, as was his custom (and it is excellent procedure too), Higgins chatted for an hour. All the while he was observing Edison, noticing the twinkle in his eye, the best expressions, the set of his mouth and typical attitudes, so that when he started shooting he might get the most characteristic poses.

Evidently he made a hit with the famous inventor. For after the sitting was over, Edison insisted that Higgins remain a while to talk some more, then for dinner, billiards after dinner, and finally overnight. Higgins rose early the next morning and hurried back to New York to process his pictures.

He got to his laboratory, grabbed a handful of 5 by 7 holders and went into the developing room. Then as he pulled out slides, he almost died. Every holder was empty. He grabbed another batch; more empty holders. Finally he picked up the last two holders in his case. Fortunately there was film in them and they developed into excellent negatives.

It seems that in the excitement to rush out on the job Higgins picked up a dozen empty holders instead of the dozen loaded for the assignment. By good luck a couple of loaded holders were in his case.

As it turned out, those two lone shots were very, very good. One was used for the *American*'s story. Later, when Edison died, the magazine received more than a hundred requests from utility companies all over the United States for photographic copies of the picture.

To wind up this chapter, we will pass along some advice from one of the leading news photographers of the United States—Joe Costa, photo supervisor of King Features-*Sunday Mirror* Magazine. From his article in the *Complete Book of Press Photography,* we quote the eleven rules he sets up to guide news photographers and some of the remarks he makes to back up his advice. Though directed primarily at the news professional, Joe's instructions should aid everyone who wants to make pictures for publication.

Let's start with his eleven rules:

1. Know your story so all the facts are assembled in your mind.
2. Big images have impact—get in close and fill up the negative.
3. Know your camera so well that it almost works as an automatic part of you. This will leave your mind entirely free to concentrate on your subjects and your pictures, not the mechanics of shooting.
4. Heads and hands are dominantly important—don't overlook them.
5. In groups, get your people close together—it will result in larger faces and better features in the picture.
6. Get on the scene as early as possible—survey—think—find best locations—props—backgrounds. Eliminate clutter—simplify.
7. Get acquainted with your people fast—get them to like you and work *with* you, not *for* you.
8. "One more" makes good sense. In spite of all the ribbing cameramen take about the inevitable "one more"—it is often that "one more" exposure which captures the best expression to better tell the story.
9. Consider your lighting. How can it be used to aid the picture?
10. Never make a picture with one flash bulb if you have time to use two or more.
11. If you must use only one bulb—try to get it off the camera to achieve the greatest amount of modeling.

Before we pass along Costa's observations on "pictures with story-telling impact," we would like to discuss his rule number two. It is agreed that big images on the negative are fine most of the time, but not as a 100 percent proposition. There may be times when you are working under specific instructions from the assigning editor. Then, of course, it's up to you to produce what he asks for, whether it be big images or small.

But when you are shooting on your own the problem is different. You must give editors leeway in judging your offerings. That calls for variety. Fill up some of your negatives. But don't fill up all of them. Get some of the surroundings and identifying background into your pictures. And leave a little air for editors and artists to play with. Elsewhere we have pointed out the necessity for that and have cautioned against too close cropping both in making the original negative and in printing enlargements.

Now let's get back to Costa and see what else he has to say:

"The photographer who makes the most effective use of his props and subjects to produce complete story-telling pictures will, therefore, command the greatest attention and remuneration.

"For those of us already working in press photography and those planning careers in this fascinating, glamorous profession, it is important that we continually analyze and consider how to use the tools at our disposal (cameras, light, situations, props, and, above all, people) to make our pictures tell their story in the most effective, complete, and convincing way."

Joe goes on: "Placing the principals in settings that identify story and locale is the simplest and most often used technique in making story-telling pictures.

"An example of such a picture is the one of Errol Flynn taken when he was involved in an early-morning argument with a taxi-driver and a New York City policeman. The cameraman covering that story had many opportunities to shoot pictures of Flynn. But the one which best told the story of Flynn's escapade was the picture which showed him against a background sign with the arrow pointing to the 'Prison Pen' where prisoners are detained awaiting their turn in court.

"In the same sense pictures of well-known personalities, of themselves alone, are not necessarily story-telling pictures. But a picture of a President or well-known figure wearing an Indian headdress or in any other situation which directly identifies him with the story being covered comes under the same category as the Flynn picture.

"In connection with pictures of prominent, well-known personalities, it is not always necessary to show their faces. For example, there were many pictures made of the late Fiorello LaGuardia that did not show his face. He was such a photogenic subject and his short, rotund little figure and black hat were so well known to newspaper readers, that on many occasions press photographers made pictures of him from the side or from the rear. This technique places the emphasis on the other people or the background in the picture which better illustrated the story in which the mayor figured.

"The picture by Nat Fein of the New York *Herald Tribune* showing Babe Ruth's last appearance on a baseball field had so much story-telling punch that it won a Pulitzer Prize for the photographer."

Because Joe was writing, in the main, for professionals familiar with that picture, he did not explain that Fein's shot was a rear view of the Babe. Taken on Babe Ruth Day, only a few months before Ruth's death, it showed his fellow ball-players lined up at the right and the filled stands of Yankee Stadium in the background. Dominating the foreground was the bowed back of the once mighty Babe, the uniform with the big "3" sagging on his disease-wasted body but the stance of the now frail legs still unmistakable.

Right here we might add that one year Wide World Photos ran a series of Famous Backs, showing rear views of the famous and not so famous. The suggestion for that series came from Kent Cooper, executive director of the AP.

Costa has a few more quotes worth remembering. File them away in your mental notebook, ready to be brought out and applied when needed. Here they are:

> Simplicity in pictures is something for which we should always strive. For instance, to tell the story that is Fall, it is not always necessary to shoot a scene of a forest showing the half-bare limbs of the trees. A picture of a child or a girl holding a single dried leaf or a twig with several dried leaves would tell the story—create the impression—just as effectively.
>
> Similarly, a close-up picture of a ruddy-faced, healthy, smiling girl with a few small splotches of snow on her face and hair tells the story of snow and winter just as effectively as a large landscape of a winter scene. And *above all* getting people and personalities in your pictures makes them more attractive and eye-compelling.

Joe also gives some useful tips on lighting and the use of flash bulbs. The importance of lighting cannot be overemphasized, but let's listen to Costa:

> Lighting can be one of our biggest assets in creating storytelling pictures. Used properly, it can aid the mood the picture is intended to convey.
>
> A front light produces a sameness of tone and flatness of quality, which makes pictures taken in this manner, at the very best, good for documentary purposes only.
>
> Lighting that helped convey the story is the back-lighted scene, the interior of a Pan American Constellation, showing sleeping passengers during a transoceanic night flight. Front lighting would not have conveyed the feeling of nighttime and the feeling of sleep, even though the people were shown in identically the same postures.

His concluding statement sums up his code:

> Pictures can be made to tell part of a story, can be made to distort the truth, or even tell an outright lie. Therefore, if we are to ever achieve the recognition for public service that is rightfully due us, if we want the public to regard press photography as one of the most important mediums of public information and education, we must never fail to be honest in our photo reporting. Make every effort to tell as honest, accurate, and complete a story as it is in your power to tell.

Let that be the code of everyone aspiring to make pictures for publication.

This is the famous Winecoff Hotel fire photograph that won the Pulitzer Prize for Arnold Hardy. *For his own account of the making and selling of this picture, turn to page 184.* *An Associated Press photo.*

An amateur made this famous picture of the Vestris *disaster in which 113 persons lost their lives. Details will be found on page 183. N. Y.* Daily News *photo, copyright News Syndicate Co., Inc.*

Luck was bountiful when Max Peter Haas literally walked into his beat on the Esposito (mad dog) killings in midtown Manhattan. For details, including how he marketed the picture and is still selling it, *turn to page 189.* *Photo copyright Max Peter Haas.*

Seconds from eternity. Fingers were releasing their grip on the Empire State Building as the shutter snapped and the suicide dropped to his death. Details of the making and marketing of this remarkable photograph will be found on pages 110-111. *A New York* Mirror *photo.*

This shot of the Staten Island Ferry Terminal fire stretched across six columns in the New York Journal-American *on June 25, 1946. The picture shows the original crop marks. Bob Keogh,* J-A *assignment editor, tells the story of this amateur lucky strike on page 116. Photo courtesy of R. F. Keogh and the* Journal-American.

There is an affinity between free-lance photographers and the Empire State Building. R. C. Wiles of Eden, Maryland, made this photograph and Life *published it. Details start on page 134. Photo by R. C. Wiles.*

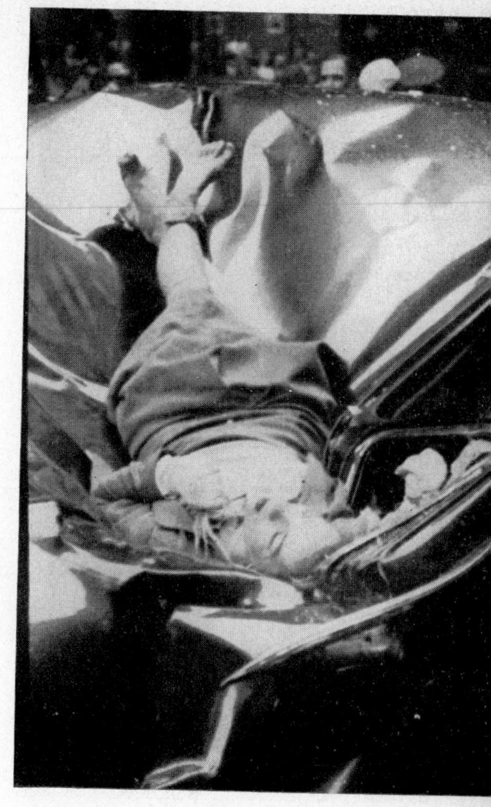

Opposite

Top: The pilot stayed dry but the photographer got wet. Frank Seed waded out to make his series of shots of the helicopter rescue. He did a good selling job, too. See page 12. Bottom: This is the helicopter rescue picture that interested a rope manufacturer. Turn to page 153 in the chapter "The 'Little' Markets." Photographs from Frank O. Seed, Niagara Falls, New York.

The progress of an eclipse of the moon was recorded on a single piece of film in this remarkable photograph. Details are on pages 170-172. Photo by Frank Jones of the Twin City Sentinel, *Winston-Salem, North Carolina.*

Seeding the desert from the air, with a man on horseback as guide. Details of the making and marketing of this feature series are on page 33. Photo by Charles W. Herbert, Western Ways, Tucson, Arizona.

A ship in every slip. This picture keeps selling steadily. It was the result of careful planning, not luck. For details, see page 173. Photo by Charles Phelps Cushing, New York.

The church by the roadside. Ability to recognize a good composition makes this photograph a best-seller. *Turn to page 173 for details.* *Photo by Charles Phelps Cushing, New York.*

This bull elephant was on his hind legs all ready to charge if the airplane got any lower. For details, see page 58. Photo by Aero Service Corporation, Philadelphia, Pennsylvania.

Opposite

How to do it and how not to do it. Joe Costa demonstrates the technique of picturing sleep in an airplane. Top is wrong; bottom is the right way. The secret of the difference is in the placing of the lights, as told on page 182. New York Sunday Mirror *photos.*

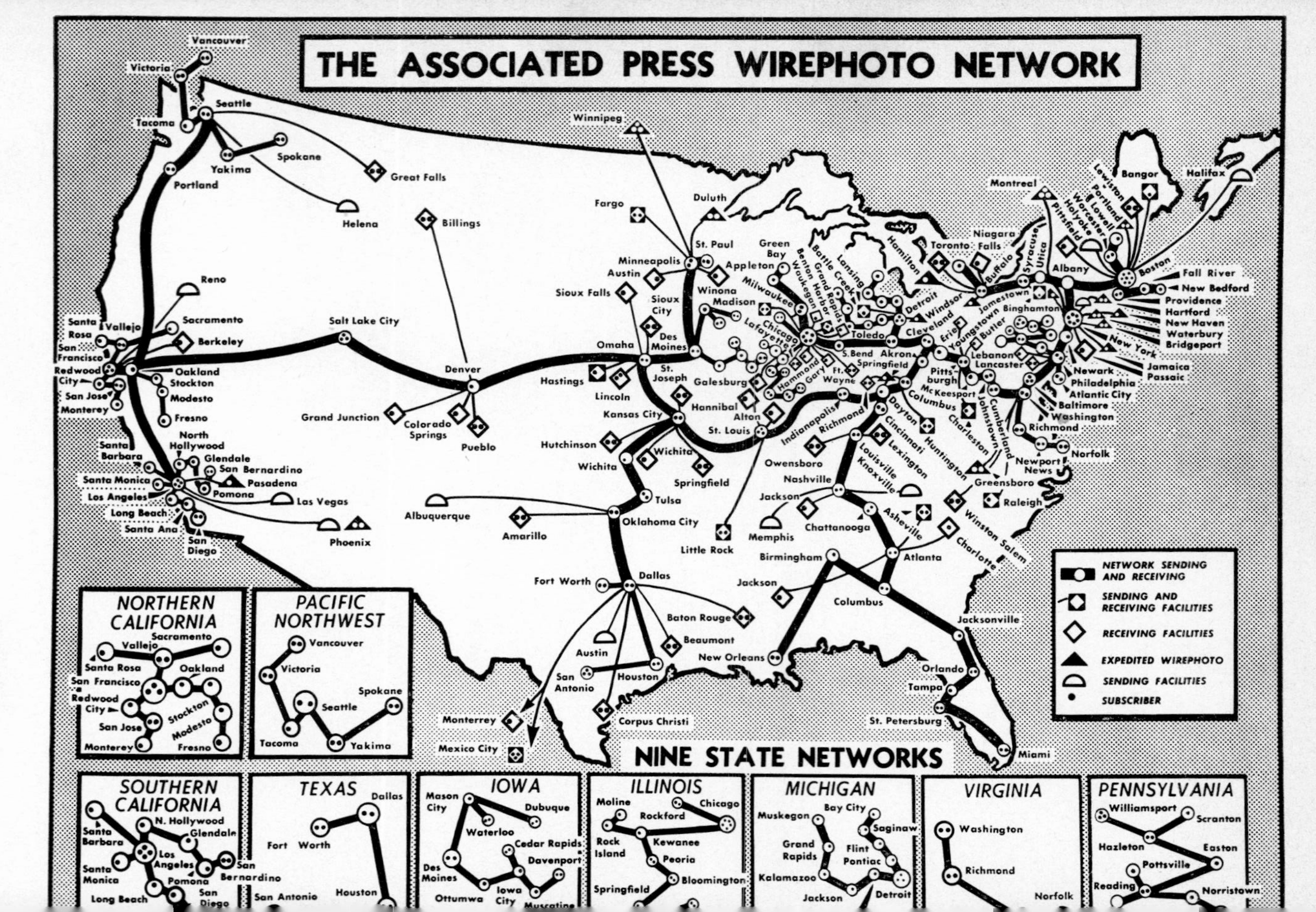

THE ASSOCIATED PRESS WIREPHOTO NETWORK
NETWORK SENDING AND RECEIVING
SENDING AND RECEIVING FACILITIES
RECEIVING FACILITIES
EXPEDITED WIREPHOTO
SENDING FACILITIES
SUBSCRIBER
Vancouver
Victoria
Seattle
Tacoma
Yakima
Spokane
Portland
Great Falls
Helena
Billings
Reno
Sacramento
Vallejo
Santa Rosa
San Francisco
Redwood City
San Jose
Monterey
Berkeley
Oakland
Stockton
Modesto
Fresno
Salt Lake City
Denver
Grand Junction
Colorado Springs
Pueblo
Santa Barbara
North Hollywood
Glendale
San Bernardino
Pasadena
Pomona
Santa Monica
Los Angeles
Long Beach
Santa Ana
San Diego
Las Vegas
Phoenix
Albuquerque
Amarillo
Winnipeg
Fargo
Duluth
St. Paul
Minneapolis
Austin
Sioux Falls
Sioux City
Des Moines
Omaha
Hastings
Lincoln
St. Joseph
Kansas City
Hutchinson
Wichita
Tulsa
Oklahoma City
Springfield
Little Rock
Fort Worth
Dallas
Austin
San Antonio
Houston
Corpus Christi
Monterrey
Mexico City
Beaumont
Baton Rouge
New Orleans
Jackson
Memphis
Green Bay
Appleton
Winona
Madison
Milwaukee
Waukegan
Benton Harbor
Grand Rapids
Battle Creek
Lansing
Chicago
Lafayette
Galesburg
Hammond
Gary
Hannibal
Alton
St. Louis
S. Bend
Ft. Wayne
Indianapolis
Richmond
Springfield
Toledo
Akron
Detroit
Windsor
Hamilton
Toronto
Niagara Falls
Buffalo
Cleveland
Erie
Youngstown
Butler
Jamestown
Pittsburgh
McKeesport
Columbus
Dayton
Cincinnati
Lexington
Louisville
Knoxville
Owensboro
Nashville
Chattanooga
Asheville
Birmingham
Atlanta
Columbus
Huntington
Charleston
Johnstown
Cumberland
Lebanon
Lancaster
Syracuse
Utica
Binghamton
Albany
Montreal
Pittsfield
Holyoke
Worcester
Lowell
Portland
Lewiston
Bangor
Halifax
Boston
Fall River
New Bedford
Providence
Hartford
New Haven
Waterbury
Bridgeport
New York
Jamaica
Passaic
Newark
Philadelphia
Atlantic City
Baltimore
Washington
Richmond
Norfolk
Newport News
Greensboro
Raleigh
Winston Salem
Charlotte
Jacksonville
Orlando
Tampa
St. Petersburg
Miami
NINE STATE NETWORKS
NORTHERN CALIFORNIA
Sacramento
Vallejo
Santa Rosa
Oakland
San Francisco
Redwood City
Stockton
San Jose
Modesto
Monterey
Fresno
PACIFIC NORTHWEST
Vancouver
Victoria
Spokane
Seattle
Tacoma
Yakima
SOUTHERN CALIFORNIA
N. Hollywood
Santa Barbara
Glendale
Los Angeles
San Bernardino
Santa Monica
Pomona
Long Beach
San Diego
TEXAS
Dallas
Fort Worth
San Antonio
Houston
IOWA
Mason City
Dubuque
Waterloo
Cedar Rapids
Davenport
Des Moines
Ottumwa
Iowa City
ILLINOIS
Moline
Chicago
Rockford
Rock Island
Kewanee
Peoria
Springfield
Bloomington
MICHIGAN
Bay City
Muskegon
Saginaw
Grand Rapids
Flint
Pontiac
Kalamazoo
Jackson
Detroit
VIRGINIA
Washington
Richmond
Norfolk
PENNSYLVANIA
Williamsport
Scranton
Hazleton
Easton
Pottsville
Reading
Norristown

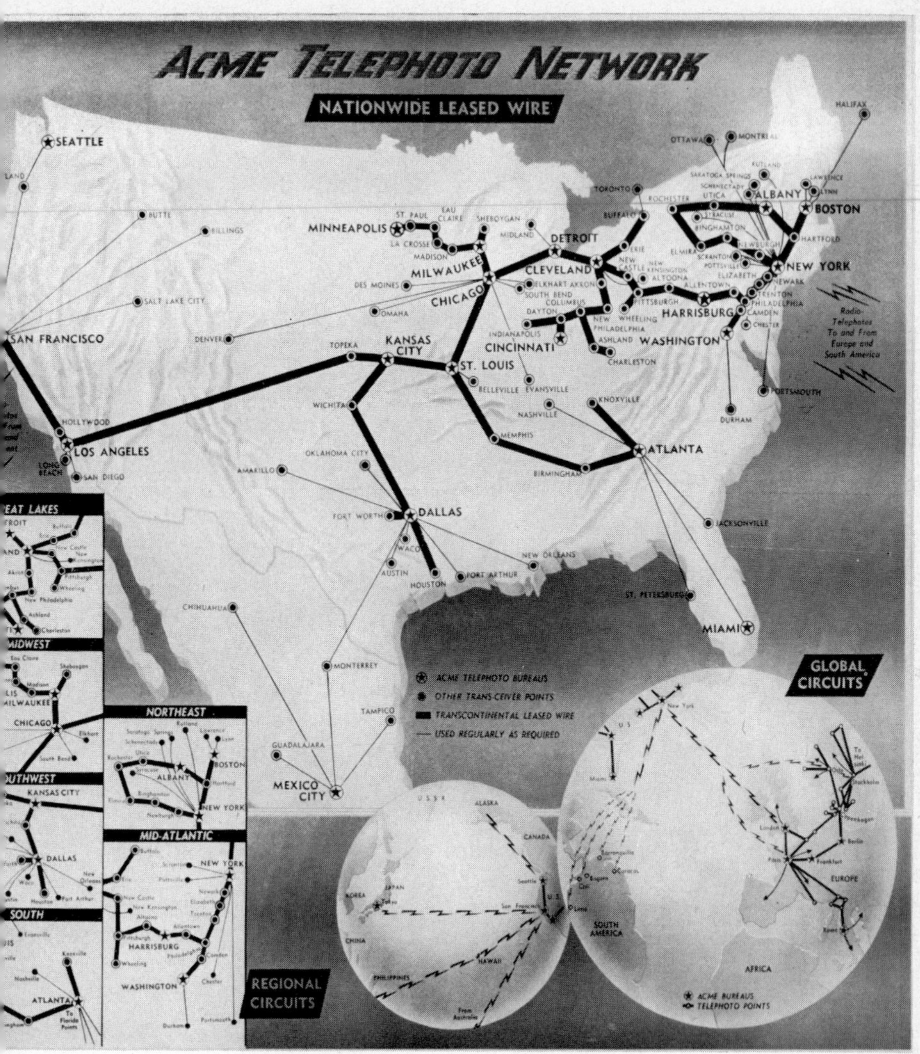

Acme Telephoto Network, including regional and global circuits.

Opposite

The Associated Press Wirephoto Network, showing in detail nine State networks.

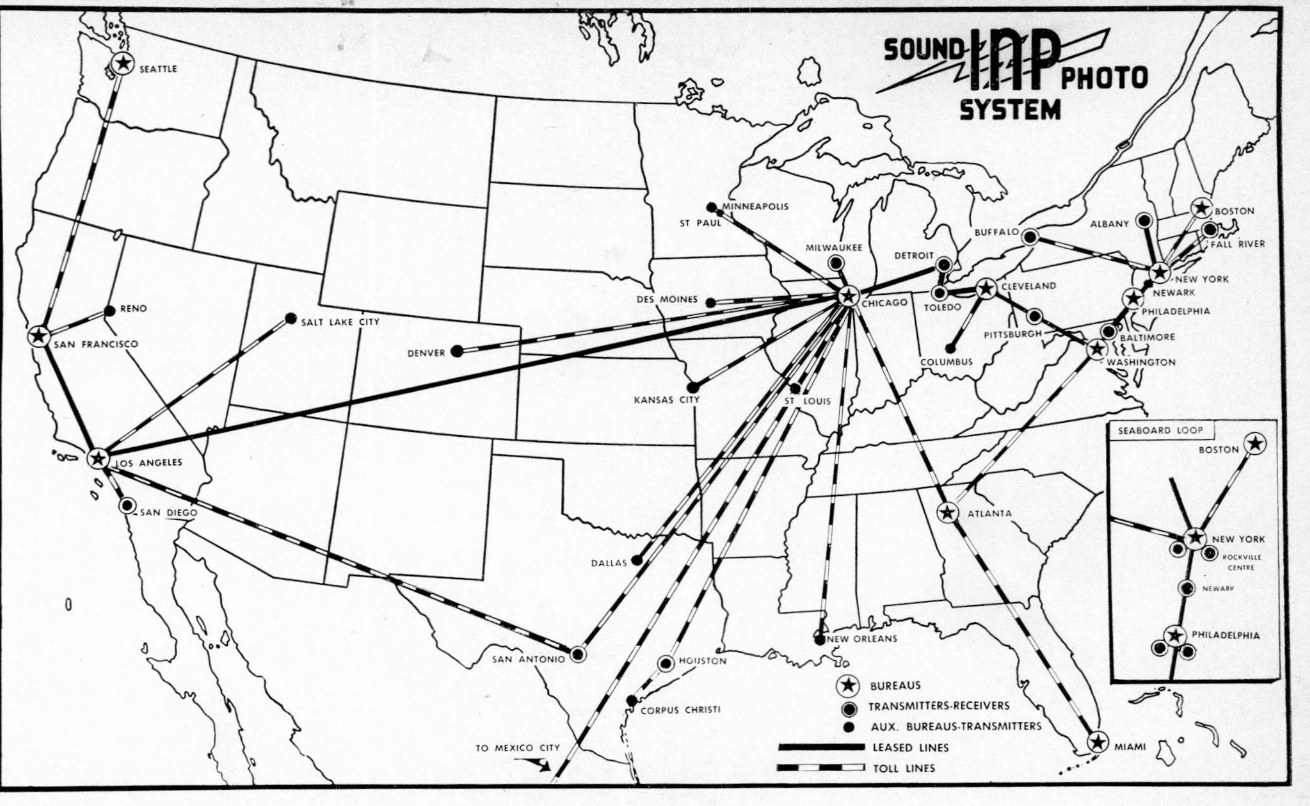

INP Sound Photo System.

They Were There When News Was Breaking

WHENEVER EDITORS REMINISCE about picture beats, the sinking of the S.S. *Vestris* usually gets first mention. Everyone we questioned about amateur photos of more than fleeting prominence responded with: "You remember the *Vestris* picture, don't you?"

We do and so does everybody else who read daily newspapers more than twenty years ago. Bound from New York to South America, the British vessel foundered in a storm off the Virginia Capes in 1928, with a loss of 110 lives. For sheer dramatic story telling, nothing has exceeded that shot of the distracted passengers running about on the sloping deck of the sinking ship. Though I haven't seen a copy of the photograph in many years, the picture is still clear in memory.

An amateur made that picture. The cameraman lucky enough to be on the spot was Fred Hanson, at that time a member of the *Vestris* crew—a pantryman in fact. And he didn't have any trouble selling his photograph. When the rescue vessels with the *Vestris* survivors aboard pulled into New York Harbor, cameramen and reporters swarmed aboard. Martin McEvilly of the New York *News* reached Hanson. Hanson got $500 in bills and McEvilly got his roll of film. The next day after the picture was printed, the late Captain Patterson, then publisher of the *News*, ordered his staff to find Hanson and give him another $500.

Where Hanson is now and whether he is still taking pictures for fun, the *News* couldn't tell us. On the tenth anniversary of the sinking in 1938 the paper looked him up. By that time he had left the sea and was living in Brooklyn, New York, and was employed as a structural steelworker.

Among more recent spot-news jackpots, the one hit by Arnold

E. Hardy ranks very high. At the start of this book we mentioned his picture scoop at the Winecoff Hotel fire in Atlanta, Georgia, in 1946. At that time he was a student at Georgia Tech. Now he lives and works in Shreveport, Louisiana.

We have heard many tales about how Hardy happened to be at the right spot at the right time to make his famous picture of a woman falling from the flaming hotel. We also have heard various tales of how he sold the pictures and the total he received from all sources. They were all good stories but they didn't match. So we wrote to Hardy. Here is his own account of that picture exploit:

"On the night of Friday, December 6th," writes Hardy, "I had been out dancing and upon returning to my room, about a mile from downtown Atlanta, I decided to stay up a while and study. About quarter to four, as I started undressing for bed, I began to hear fire sirens in the distance. Soon they could be heard from every direction, heading for the downtown section of Atlanta. On the hunch that it might be a large store or warehouse, I phoned the fire department and asked where it was. They told me the Winecoff Hotel. I phoned a taxi, grabbed my camera, and started running for town. About three blocks down I met my cab and flagged it. I reached the hotel at four o'clock, only a little while after the fire had started.

"Flames were raging in the sixth, seventh, eighth, and ninth floors, and in almost every window from the fourth floor up to the top, men, women, and children were waving and screaming for help. I offered to help the firemen but they said they had all the volunteers they could use. Since I could be of no help, I started shooting pictures. I was using Kodak Super XX film which helped immensely, but if you've ever thought of lighting a sixteen-story building with one midget flash bulb, you know what I was up against. I was using G.E. No. 5 bulbs which I thought were only for short-range shots.

"Setting my camera at 1/50th second at *f/4.5* focused at infinity, I fired two shots straight up the wall, and later, when I processed my film, both shots were good. That building was lighted for sixteen stories straight up in both shots. Climbing over hose, dodging firemen, ambulances, and falling debris, my camera was accidently struck, firing the flash gun and wasting a precious bulb. On my next shot I pulled one of the oldest boners known to photographers—I forgot to cock the shutter. That really hurt, but I had one bulb left and I was determined to make it count.

"By now the trapped victims," Hardy continues, "had started descending ropes of sheets and blankets in a desperate attempt to reach the fire-ladders which reached to only the eighth floor. Every minute or so, a rope would break and a man or woman would plunge eight or ten stories to the street below. Some, driven to desperation by flames in their rooms, would jump from their windows rather than burn to death. I felt that if I could bring the horror of that scene before the public, it would stir them to the point where they would demand that hotels and other public buildings install better safety measures.

"I had a miniature Speed Graphic upon which I had rigged up my own synchronizer by redesigning a regular solenoid. I had completed it only a week before and had never run a synchronization test on it. I had shot a few pictures at 1/100th second which came out all right, so I didn't bother to check it at higher speeds, thinking I would have no immediate need for high speeds. Now I needed high speed and needed it badly.

"I set my shutter at 1/400th second at *f/4.5* focused at 50 feet and waited. Just as I completed the settings I heard the women behind me shriek. I looked up, raising my camera as I did. A woman was plummeting downward. I managed to spot her in the view finder and followed her down. As she passed the third floor window I fired. A fire-truck stood between me and the building, and momentarily blinded by the flash, I lost sight of her. It is my belief that she struck the edge of the marquee, then dropped to the ground. I never saw her again.

"From then on I could do nothing but watch and shoot an occasional time exposure of the flames pouring out of the windows. The bodies continued to fall. I counted at least fifteen drop in half an hour's time. Several photographers fired at them as they fell, so I knew that my shot would merely be a repetition of their shots. On the chance that I *might* have something different, I rushed out to Georgia Tech, where I could get the use of a darkroom. While the negatives were drying, I called the Associated Press to see if they would be interested. When I described what I had, they asked me to bring the pictures down. When they looked at the negatives they said they would like to buy them and asked what I would take. I had no idea what to ask, so finally they made an offer of $150. I figured if they would offer that, they would pay more, so I asked for $300. They hesitated for a few minutes, then accepted. The next day they called me and gave me a $200 bonus. I signed away all rights to the pictures, including prizes; however the Associated Press entered my picture of the woman falling in a number of contests and gave me all the prizes.

"The prizes consisted of:

1. *Editor & Publisher* Award for No. 1 news shot of the year—$150.
2. First prize in the *Encyclopaedia Britannica* Annual Contests—$100 and a set of the encyclopaedias.
3. First prize in Kent (Ohio) State University's Annual Photography contest—$40.
4. The Graflex Diamond Award—A gold key set with a diamond.
5. A Distinguished Service Award Special Citation from Sigma Delta Chi, Professional Journalistic Society.
6. Pulitzer Prize in Journalism from Columbia University—$500.

"My camera is a 2¼ by 3¼ Anniversary Model Miniature Speed Graphic and is equipped with an *f/4.5* Graflex Optar 101 coated lens in a Graflex shutter. All shots were made with the between-the-lens shutter.

"Photography has been a hobby of mine for about thirteen years, during which time I progressed from a $15 Argus to a Kodak Monitor 620 and then to my present 2¼ by 3¼ Speed Graphic, which I purchased about a month before the Winecoff fire.

"My interest in photography has been mostly in portrait work, dramatic lighting effects, silhouettes, and the like. Though photography holds a keen fascination for me, I never expect to follow it as a profession, as my main interest is in the field of physics."

Without taking into consideration anything but cash, Hardy's night's work brought him $1,290. That's not at all bad for losing a few hours' sleep.

And it seems when a photographer is destined to hit a spot-news jackpot, otherwise fatal sins of omission and commission don't count. From his own story Hardy tackled his biggest picture job with incompletely tested equipment and made mistakes that wasted bulbs. In spite of that he "got the picture" and, though he didn't reach the AP Atlanta bureau until hours after the first fire pictures had been transmitted, his photos stole the play all over the country.

Another amateur-produced beat handled by the AP is still remembered in its New York office. On April 26, 1941, M. Spitalnick, a free-lance photographer, came in with some negatives of an automobile accident at 57th Street and Madison Avenue. He had been passing that corner when a car knocked down and seriously injured a pedestrian. Spitalnick had shot the scene but for some reason had not learned the name of the injured man. The editors accepted his pictures as good shots of what, from a news point of view, appeared to be a minor accident.

After the photographer left his negatives and before the desk had had time to order prints for its member papers, the office received a flash that the noted violinist Fritz Kreisler had been hit and seriously injured at the 57th Street corner. That provided the necessary identification for Spitalnick's pictures. They immediately soared in value to the AP, which Wirephotoed them as the written story was moving on other wires. And the photographer got a much larger payment than that promised for just-another-accident picture.

Rescues at sea and plane and balloon crashes at isolated spots no longer seem to result in the picture bonanzas they once yielded to amateurs. Perhaps styles in news pictures change; perhaps the pattern of news breaks is different today. Whatever the cause, such accidents used to provide spot-news thrills and cash for free-lances and amateurs; they may do so again. It was free-lances who cleaned up when Will Rogers and Wiley Post died in the crash of their plane at Point Barrow, Alaska, in 1935. Local free-lances also made the pictures when the ill-fated Navy dirigible *Shenandoah,* on a flight over the Middle West, fell apart near Avon, Ohio, on September 3, 1925.

Both American and German sailors with cameras made money when the Nazis scuttled the North German Lloyd's third biggest luxury liner, the *Columbus,* off the Delaware Capes on December 19, 1939. At the war's start, the 32,581-ton cruise ship had been in Curaçao, Dutch West Indies, with 745 American passengers aboard. On September 1, the day Germany invaded Poland, her skipper, Captain Wilhelm Daehne, dumped his passengers at Havana, then took his vessel to the neutral refuge of Veracruz, Mexico. In December the captain and his crew upped anchor for a perilous sneak trip home. As the vessel proceeded through the Gulf and up the United States coast, the British destroyer *Hyperion* picked up her trail and followed, waiting for her to move out of U.S. territorial waters. The United States heavy cruiser *Tuscaloosa,* Captain Harry A. Badt commanding, was also there to see that neutrality was not violated. Suddenly the German skipper radioed the *Tuscaloosa* that he was about to scuttle his ship, asked if the American vessel, with its crew of five hundred fifty, had room for the German crew of nearly six hundred, and, as the British destroyer fired across the *Columbus's* bow, ordered his men into the boats and with gasoline turned his ship into an inferno. With a loss of only two lives, the *Tuscaloosa* rescued 567 German survivors and brought them to Ellis Island in New York Harbor.

At that time privately owned cameras were banned on American naval vessels. Any brought aboard were impounded until the ships returned to port. When Captain Badt saw that the *Columbus* was being scuttled and her crew was taking to the boats, he temporarily lifted the camera ban. He permitted sailors owning cameras to get them out of custody and to make pictures of the sinking and the rescue operations. Most of the photographs obtained by press associations and newspapers were made by American sailors. Some were sold at Quarantine to reporters and cameramen who went down the bay to meet the *Tuscaloosa* and get stories and pictures from rescuers and survivors. Other American sailors waited until they could get ashore and take their films directly to newspaper and syndicate offices.

There was at least one set of photographs that were not American. Acme sent Ben Handel, then one of its editors and now a picture editor at the New York *News*, to Quarantine to check the German sailors for pictures. First he found a German seaman who could speak English. For a twenty-dollar bill the sailor became Handel's interpreter and helped him in the search for a picture-taking German. They found one who had shot a roll of films. Handel bought the undeveloped roll for $100. That sight-unseen buy turned out to be a lucky bargain. Some of the best pictures of the *Columbus* scuttling—the men scrambling down the side of the smoking ship and pulling off in lifeboats—were on that roll of film.

For cash returns and pure luck in being there at the right time, Max Peter Haas ranks high on the list of photographers who have hit the jackpot. He made the pictures when the so-called "mad dog" killers, Anthony and William Esposito, staged a twenty-minute gun battle all around B. Altman's department store, across the street from the Empire State Building in New York. During it they killed two men, including the traffic policeman at 34th Street and Fifth Avenue, and wounded two others before they were battered into submission by police and an enraged noon-hour crowd. Hoodlums with a long record of arrests for robbery and gun-law violations, they feigned madness in an unsuccessful attempt to escape the chair.

As we have mentioned earlier in this book, Haas profited partly from preparedness and partly from luck: the shooting took place outside the building in which Haas has his office; it occurred just as he stepped out of the door with the Leica that he always carries. To date he estimates that he has cleared more than $4,000 from the Esposito pictures.

Although Haas is a professional who operates his own photo agency, to a great extent every amateur and free-lance can copy his marketing procedure: he sold the first rights to the pictures to what he felt would be the best-paying customer for them; since then he has made as many repeat sales as possible. It was to the *Daily News* that he first took his minicam film; he was reasonably certain that it would pay highest for that sort of spot news. He has a knowledge and "feel" of the market that, of course, comes from his being in the photo-selling business. That his later returns were large is probably also the result of his being in the business; running his own picture agency gives Haas a chance to make the repeat sales the amateur and the independent free-lance either misses entirely or makes only through sales by an agent who collects half of every payment.

We have cited several instances where delay in getting pictures to market has not been a fatal error. Nevertheless, dawdling, whether it be but a few hours or as much as a day, isn't recommended. The photographer who takes his time is flirting with the chance of ringing up No Sale. Such an experience is recalled by Frank Seed.

The Bridal Veil Falls are part of Seed's daily beat in making pictures of honeymooners and other visitors to Niagara Falls, New York. One morning he reached that spot a few moments after a visitor had plunged to his death over the brink of the Falls. One of the policemen stationed in the area told Seed the news and pointed out a tourist who had snapped his shutter as the suicide's body fell. Seed hurried over to the amateur.

"Did you get a shot of that suicide?" he asked. "I certainly did," was the reply. "I caught him just as his body turned over in midair." Noticing that the man was carrying a 2¼ by 3¼ Graphic, an excellent outfit for making action shots, Seed offered $50 sight unseen for his exposed film.

The amateur thought a moment and then said "No." Seed raised the bid to $100, with the proviso that they go back to the studio first, and develop the film. If the picture was good, the exchange of $100 for the negative would be made then and there. There was still no sale, so Seed asked why.

"Well," said the photographer, "if that picture is worth $100 to you, I'll take it back home and sell it myself for more." "Where do you live," countered Seed, "and when do you expect to get back home?" "St. Louis and in ten days," was the final reply.

So far as Frank Seed knows, that shot of a suicide at Niagara Falls is still unsold. In fact he would have been very much surprised to see it in print. Though he could not convince the amateur of the need for marketing speed, Seed knows that spot-news pictures are most perishable items.

On the day of the suicide, Seed was certain, the picture syndicate for which he was stringer correspondent would have backed him up on the purchase. That day the photo was very valuable, because it could be transmitted while the news was fresh. Seed knew, too, that a day later it would still have some news value, but the selling price would be nearer $5 than $100. Ten days later and from St. Louis, its news value would be entirely gone. It would be just another vacation picture to be pasted in an album or submitted to a local camera contest.

Sometimes it pays the amateur photographer to let newspapers and agencies gamble on sight-unseen purchases. It is true that an after-seeing offer may bring greater returns if there is something extra good on your negatives. But if you are not sure of your photography, that's a big risk. If you develop your negatives before offering them and the pictures turn out to be poor, out of focus, undertimed, you may get very little or nothing at all.

Joseph J. Wurzel, now picture editor of *Look,* was one of the principals in a transaction whereby the amateur photographer profited handsomely by accepting a before-development offer. The incident occurred more than twenty years ago, when Wurzel was European picture manager for the Associated Press.

Off the coast of South America, the liner *Principessa Mafalda* was wrecked and sank. The freighter *Empire Star,* bound for London, helped in the rescue efforts. According to reports reaching London before the freighter made port, the first engineer had made pictures during the rescue operations.

Naturally, when the *Empire Star* steamed up the Thames to London, alert newsmen boarded her. One of them was Joe. By the time he found the first engineer's cabin, a London *Times* reporter was already in conversation with that ship's officer.

Seemingly the deal had been closed, but Wurzel, seeking an opening, interposed a "hope you got a good round sum for your film." It was 120 millimeter. Then he asked about light conditions and how far away the engineer was from the wreck when he made his pictures. Satisfied that there was a chance that some of the exposures would be printable and not knowing how much the *Times* man had offered, Wurzel bid £15 (at that time the equivalent of almost $75) for the roll of film sight unseen.

The engineer turned to the London *Times* reporter to see whether he would raise his offer. He couldn't but suggested that they take the roll to the *Times* office, develop it, and then, after inspection, make another offer. Wurzel started counting out crisp banknotes while the discussion was in progress. He won and rushed back to his office with the roll.

As it turned out, the *Empire Star*'s first engineer won the gamble. There were only two fairly good shots on the entire roll, and neither was worth anywhere near $75.

From the very start, the value of speed in marketing news pictures has been emphasized. Sometimes speed is so important that much more money is spent on delivering the pictures than in buying them.

It wasn't too long ago, in the days before pictures could be transmitted over telephone lines, that trains and planes were chartered to get pictures to the newspapers. Special planes flew the Dempsey-Gibbons fight pictures from Shelby, Montana, to New York, to the great profit of the syndicate whose plane arrived first. Those same pictures, or perhaps it was some other top picture story, went to Boston by specially chartered train to catch editions. And not quite so long ago, before transatlantic flying became commonplace, a chartered plane brought the first pictures of the coronation of King George to New York from England.

An outstanding example of delivery costs reaching very high figures is recounted by Wurzel in telling how the Associated Press got the first pictures of the death of Princess Astrid of Belgium to London. She was the first wife of the then Prince Leopold, now ex-King Leopold, of Belgium. The couple were driving through Berne, Switzerland, when their car went out of control and crashed. The princess was killed.

Wurzel realized that the pictures of the body and the wreck scene would command higher prices if they reached London that night. If he waited for routine delivery, all the competition would have pictures too, depressing prices to ordinary levels. So he telephoned the Zurich bureau of the Associated Press and instructed the editors to do two things. First he asked them to buy the first available roll of film made by a photographer on the scene. Next he told them to charter an airplane that would make a night flight to England. What the photographer received for his roll of film, Wurzel cannot recall, but he does remember that the charter fee for a three-engine plane with a crew of three was £400.

The plane reached Croyden airport about midnight. Joe was waiting as the three burly airmen, swathed in bulky flying suits, filed out of the plane. He asked the first one for the roll of film. He didn't have it. Each of the three turned to the others, asking: "Didn't you take it?" Visioning a wasted flight with the roll still in Switzerland, Wurzel started to age rapidly. But finally the suspense ended when one of the fliers put his hand deep into a pocket and brought out a tiny, two-ounce roll of film. That meant a cost of £200 per ounce—probably tops in air freight-rates for weight and distance and even at today's exchange rates a considerable sum.

Possibly the most famous shipwreck of all time occurred when the *Titanic* hit an iceberg and sank on her maiden voyage in 1912. Even then lucky passengers with cameras made money from their pictures. Of course, payments were smaller and the competition for photographs wasn't so keen and so well organized. There was a girl passenger on the *Carpathia,* which rescued some of the *Titanic* survivors, who shot a roll of film with an ordinary box camera. Sight unseen, for that practice isn't new, the late A. L. Selig, then news editor of Underwood & Underwood, bought it for $25.

Then there was the time when on the morning of October 2, 1931, Colonel Charles A. Lindbergh's plane tipped over, dunking the colonel and Mrs. Lindbergh into the Yangtze River at Hankow, China, alongside the British carrier *Hermes.* Her sailors had a field day shooting pictures of the Lindberghs' discomfort and the efforts to right the plane and hoist it back to the deck of the carrier. The pictures brought a big sum—according to the story in the New York *Times,* "one of the highest prices ever paid for pictures." But this time the cameramen on the spot didn't cash in—at least not directly.

Knowing Lindbergh's aversion to publicity, the skipper of the *Hermes* gathered up all the film and offered to destroy every shot. The colonel refused that offer and suggested that the pictures be sold to the highest bidder. Wide World Photos, Inc., won the bid, and the proceeds were used to endow a bed in the Shanghai Hospital for soldiers and sailors of all nations.

Almost every day some photographer gets a lucky break. Prices may not run into the thousands; shootings on Fifth Avenue and Winecoff Hotel fires aren't ordinary occurrences. But for the time and effort involved, the rewards are almost always very good.

Outstanding early in 1951 was the experience of William Veinfortner of Cleveland, Ohio. He was at the Philadelphia International Airport on January 14. An airliner coming in for a landing skidded off the air strip, crashed into a gully, and burst into flames. Veinfortner was less than 100 yards away. An amateur camera fan, he had his outfit along. He went into action immediately, getting the only pictures of the plane in flames and the survivors streaming out. By the time other photographers reached the scene, the airliner was a burned-out hulk. Veinfortner's pictures were printed in the Philadelphia *Bulletin* and Wirephotoed everywhere else by the Associated Press.

Having an eye for a good picture is sometimes as good as or even better than being around when spot news is breaking. Probably no one will forget the photograph of Mrs. Franklin D. Roosevelt rubbing noses with a Maori during a trip to Australia. The cameraman alert enough to catch that pose got an exclusive that is still selling.

Sometimes fate or luck, or whatever you may call it, finds rather indirect ways of leading a photographer to a hot news story. Take, for example, the last photograph made of Huey Long before his death in 1935.

As everybody knows, Long was shot to death in the State Capitol at Baton Rouge, Louisiana. Only about an hour before the fatal shooting, a Rembrandt Studio cameraman took a fine picture of the Kingfish conferring with some of the representatives before the legislature went into session. The cameraman was there because an editor of Wide World Photos in New York had seen a short dispatch in that morning's New York *Times* saying that Long would attend the Louisiana legislature's session that night. So Wide World had wired Rembrandt Studio, which was its local picture stringer correspondent, to send a man to the capitol to try for a picture of the representatives getting their orders from the state boss.

By the time the man from Rembrandt had returned to his office to process his pictures, Long was dead and his assignment was big news. What started out as a routine job worth at most a five-dollar bill had suddenly become a really hot picture story. Rembrandt kept its photos exclusive to Wide World, which, if my memory is correct, raised the payment from five to fifty dollars. The confab picture was widely used, and Wide World profited nicely from many resales.

Of course, Lady Luck cheated a bit. Had she delayed the cameraman along the way, he might have been present to record the actual shooting. But then, too, from descriptions of the scene, it is possible he also would have been shot. So maybe Lady Luck was looking out for him after all.

But it's about time to call a halt to reminiscence. We could go on and on, citing free-lance photographers lucky enough to be nearby when news was breaking—and ready for their break because they heeded the admonition you also should heed: "Keep that camera with you and keep it loaded."

Index

action pictures, 176-177
agencies, Canadian, 91
  Combine Photos, Ltd., 92
  Culver Service, 92
  European Pictures, 82-85
  Ewing Galloway, 92-93
  Graphic House, 90-91
  list of, 91
  Pix, Inc., 88-90
  Publix Pictures, 86-87
  Western Ways, 32-34, 87-88
air views, 39-64
  captions for, 47
  in color, 52
calendars, market in, 86, 156, 157
camera, equipment for, 5-6
  practice in handling, 175-176
  safeguarding, 168, 169
  and type, 5-6
  size, 17-18
captions, for air views, 47
  clearness of, 16
  completeness of, 66-67, 68, 69
  content, sample of, 70-71
  dating, 74
  for feature pictures, 71, 72-73
  importance of good, 65-66, 74
  length of, 67-68
  names in, 16
color, in air views, 52
  markets for, agency, 86, 87, 89, 95-96
  magazine, 131, 136-138, 140-141, 146, 147-149
  newspaper, 108, 111, 118, 119, 121, 123, 124, 125, 126, 127
eclipse, photographing, 170-172
feature pictures, 20-22, 32-38
  best markets for, 30-32
  captions for, 71, 72-73
  defined, 8, 21
  shape of pictures, 27, 28
  shooting script for, 22-26
feature pictures, *contd.*
  time factor in, 28-29
  variety in, 27
film, roll or cut, 17, 18
free-lance beats, Chunking bombing, 132-134
  Columbus scuttled, 9, 188-189
  Empire State Building suicides, 101, 110, 111, 134, 135
  Esposito killers, 18, 99
  Kreisler accident, 187
  Lindbergh dunked, 193, 194
  Niagara rescue, 12
  Philadelphia plane crash, 194
  Staten Island Ferry fire, 116
  Vestris sinking, 9, 183
  Winecoff Hotel fire, 12, 184-185
house organs, market in, 154-155
journals, market in, 153-154
lighting tips, 182
magazine requirements, 128-129
  American Magazine, 147, 149
  Collier's, 30, 147-148
  Holiday, 30, 140-142
  Ladies' Home Journal, 144-145
  Life, 30, 129-135
  Look, 140
  National Geographic, 135-139
  Newsweek, 129, 130
  Parade, 30, 145-146
  Saturday Evening Post, 30, 142-144
  This Week, 30, 164
  Time, 129, 130
  U. S. Camera Annual, 139-140
  Woman's Home Companion, 148-149
markets, advertising, 157-160
  calendars, 86, 156, 157
  features, 30-32
  house organs, 154, 155
  insurance companies, 156
  journals, 153-154

markets, advertising, *contd.*
magazines, 128-149
newspapers, 97-127
picture services, 75-95
publicity, 162-167
spot news, 10-19
television, 166, 167
trade papers, 153, 154
window displays, 156
mat services, 93-94
minicams, 17, 114
negatives, shipping, 14-16
newspaper requirements, 97-98
Beacon-Journal (Akron), 122
Christian Science Monitor, 123
Chronicle (San Francisco), 120
Courier-Express (Buffalo), 118
Daily Mirror (New York), 98, 99-101, 109-112
Deseret News (Salt Lake City), 124
Evening Bulletin (Providence), 126
Grit (Williamsport), 125-126
Hearst chain, 99-100
list of, 103
Herald (Boston), 126
Inquirer (Philadelphia), 119-120
Journal (Milwaukee), 122-123
Journal (Providence), 126
Journal-American (New York), 98-99, 102-103, 112-116
News (New York), 98, 104-107, 108-109
Post (Denver), 118
Post-Dispatch (St. Louis), 127
Press (Pittsburgh), 125
Register and Tribune (Des Moines), 119
Scripps-Howard chain, 103-104
list of, 104
Star (Washington), 126
Star Weekly (Toronto), 124
State Journal (Lansing), 120
Times (New York), 116-117
newspaper requirements *contd.*
Times (Seattle), 121-122
Tribune (Chicago), 124-125
Tribune (Minneapolis), 121
picture services, Acme Newspictures (United Press), 76-78
addresses, 11
Associated Press News Photos, 75-76, 94, 95
Central Press, 93-94
feature market, 31
International News Photos, 78
King Features, 94-95
Metropolitan Group Editorial Service, 79-82
Wide World Photos, 78-79
See also agencies.
prices, magazine, 131, 133, 134, 135, 137, 138
newspaper, 117, 118, 119, 120, 121, 122, 123, 124, 125, 126
prints, shapes, 27
sizes, 5
professionals, suggestions by, 168-182
publicity pictures, 162-166
releases, personal, 160, 161
repeat sales, 151-152
Rolleis, 17-18
rules for news photographers, 179
sight-unseen sales, 190-192
simplicity in pictures, 181
sports coverage, 170
spot-news pictures, 10-11, 18-19
defined, 7
developing, 14-15
exclusive sale of, 13
identifying persons in, 16
market inquiries, 11
shipping, 15-16
speed factor in selling, 13-14
telephone inquiries, 17
television, 166-167
trade papers, markets in, 153, 154